THE RUSSO-AFGHAN QUESTION

Owing to the antiquity and rarity of this book, certain pages are regrettably absent, and readability is compromised due to the blurring of the original text. If you possess any insights regarding the availability of these missing sections, kindly inform us. Your assistance is crucial in ensuring the completion of this significant work for the benefit of future generations.

THE RUSSO-AFGHAN QUESTION

AND THE INVASION OF INDIA

G. B. MALLESON

GYAN

Published by

GYAN

Gyan Publishing House
5, Ansari Road
Daryaganj, New Delhi-110002
Phone: 011-47034999, 9811692060
E-mail: books@gyanbooks.com

Distribution Network
gyanbooks.com
India, USA, Canada, UK, Australia

ISBN:978-93-7097-198-1 (PB)

First Published, 1885

2nd Impression 2025

Printed at: Gyan Press, Delhi.

THE RUSSO-AFGHAN QUESTION
Arthur G. B. MALLESON

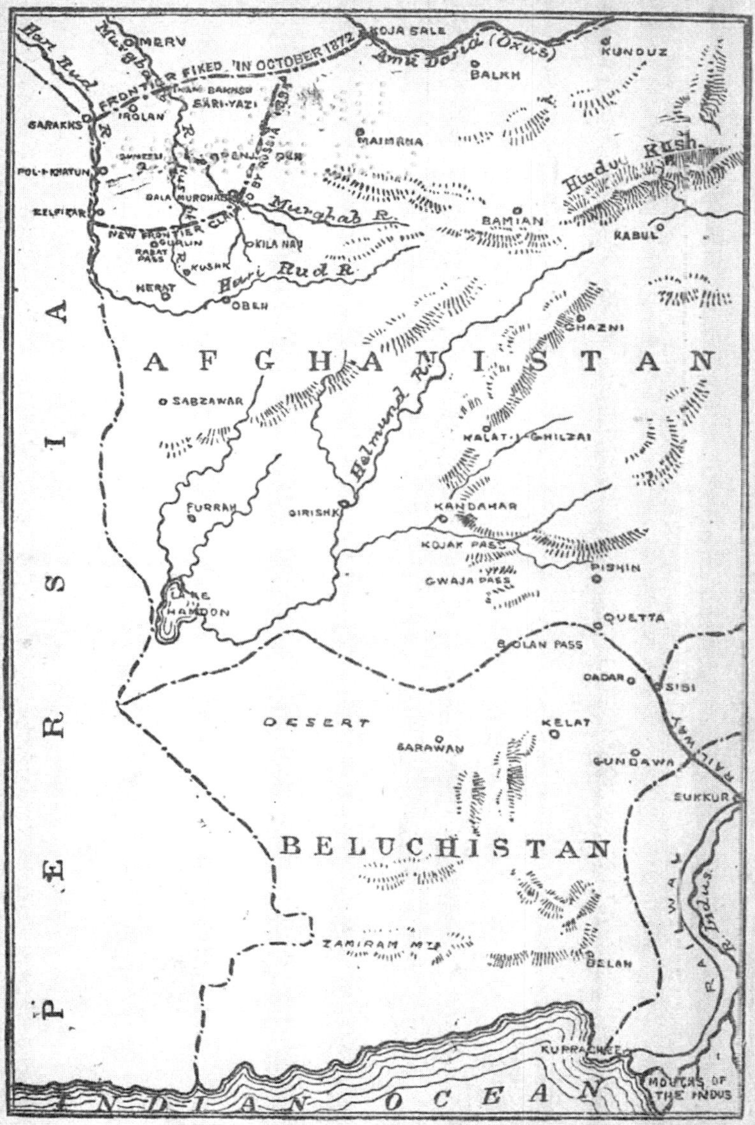

FRONTIER FIXED IN OCTOBER 1872
KOJA SALE
MERV
Amu Daria (Oxus)
KUNDUZ
BALKH
SARAKHS
IROLAN
SARI-YAZI
MAIMANA
POL-I-KHATUN
Hindu Kush
BALA MURGHAB
Murghab R.
ZULFIKAR
NEW FRONTIER CLAIMED BY RUSSIA
BAMIAN
KABUL
GURLIN
RABAT PASS
KILA NAU
KUSHK
Hari Rud R.
HERAT
OBEH
GHAZNI
AFGHANISTAN
SABZAWAR
Helmund R.
KALAT-I-GHILZAI
FURRAH
GIRISHK
KANDAHAR
KOJAK PASS
PISHIN
GWAJA PASS
LAKE HAMOON
QUETTA
BOLAN PASS
DADAR
SIBI
DESERT
KELAT
SARAWAN
GUNDAWA
SUKKUR
PERSIA
BELUCHISTAN
RAILWAY
R. Indus
ZAMIRAM MTS
BELAN
KURRACHEE
MOUTHS OF THE INDUS
INDIAN OCEAN

THE RUSSO-AFGHAN QUESTION

AND THE

INVASION OF INDIA

BY

COLONEL G. B. MALLESON, C.S.I.

AUTHOR OF "HERAT, THE GRANARY AND GARDEN OF CENTRAL ASIA," "HISTORY OF AFGHANISTAN," ETC.

SECOND EDITION

LONDON

GEORGE ROUTLEDGE AND SONS

BROADWAY, LUDGATE HILL

NEW YORK: 9 LAFAYETTE PLACE

1885

PREFACE.

RUSSIA has at last spoken! After years patiently spent in absorbing the desert, she reached in 1884 the borders of the promised land. Her first act on arriving there was to object to the frontier which Lord Granville had proposed in October, 1872, which she, by the despatches of her Chancellor, dated respectively in December, 1872, and January, 1873, had accepted, and which in Russian and English maps alike has, ever since, been marked as the frontier. Yielding, in a weak moment, to an objection posed solely for the purpose of deriving some practical advantage from the re-opening of a settled question, Lord Granville arranged with Russia that Commissioners should be sent from both countries to the spot, to fix there the exact line of demarcation which was to be the limit of Russia's advance towards India. In consequence of this agreement an English Commissioner, of distinguished service in India, proceeded without delay to the point agreed upon. He found there the valleys, the rivers, the mountains, the people, but no Russian Commissioner! The Russian Commissioner was, indeed, conspicuous by his absence, but, to counterbalance that absence, parties of Russian soldiers crossed the line which since 1872–73 had been accepted as the boundary of the country, and seized positions, useless for commercial, most important for strategical, purposes—positions which, since the year 1863, and even before that year, had paid tribute to Herát—the north-western province of the dominions of England's ally, the Amír of Afghánistán!

To show the necessity, if we wish still to hold India, of the retention, by an ally of England, of the positions Russia has seized; to demonstrate the absolute right of the Amír to those positions, and the lawlessness of the act of Russia in seizing them; to set clearly before the public the cherished ultimate aim which prompted Russia to the conquest of the desert; and to point out how the display of an iron resolution alone can avert from Herát and India the threatened danger, I have written the pages that follow. I have written them, not as a party man, but as an Englishman. Not as a party man, first, because, believing that the two great parties in the State have alike blundered, I have pointed out with impartiality the mistakes of both. Not as a party man, secondly and specially, because in a matter affecting the maintenance of an Empire the voice of patriotism should silence the selfish contentions of party. For, in very deed, it is an Empire which is now at stake, and it is by patriotic efforts alone that the splendid creation of our fathers and our fathers' fathers can be maintained.

The form in which this little book is published will make it accessible to all classes. It will tell those classes the truth, and, telling them the truth, will impose upon them a sacred duty. That duty is, above all things, to insist that the Ministers of England shall maintain, with respect to our Indian Empire, the old historical policy of England; that the Ministers of England shall compel Russia to withdraw her unjust pretensions, to retire behind the frontier which she has violated. If the people of Great Britain fail to perform this duty, they will become partners in a policy, born of infirmity of purpose and cowardice, which will lose for us our Indian Empire!

In my outspoken criticisms I may have struck at cherished prejudices and wounded personal vanities. In dealing with a crisis which is partly the consequence of mistakes in the past, it was impossible absolutely to avoid doing this. But to those who may be affected by my criticisms, and to all, I would thus appeal, using the words of the greatest of English writers: "Who is here so base that would be a bondsman? If any, speak; for him have I offended. Who is here so rude that would not be a Briton? If any, speak; for him have I offended. Who is here so vile that will not love his country? If any, speak; for him have I offended. I pause for a reply."

G. B. MALLESON.

27, WEST CROMWELL ROAD,
28 *March*, 1885.

CONTENTS.

THE

RUSSO-AFGHAN QUESTION.

CHAPTER I.

INTRODUCTORY.—GEOGRAPHICAL AND STATISTICAL.

AFGHÁNISTÁN, the land of the Afgháns, is the borderland, the frontier bulwark, of the empire of the Mogols, as that empire was constituted when the earlier princes of that race ruled India. It is bordered on the east by the Panjáb, on the south by Balúchistán, on the west by Persian Khorásán and the desert of Baksu, on the north and north-west by a line drawn from Sarakhs, just above Robat-Abdullah Khán and Andkhoi, to Khoja Saleh on the Oxus, and from the latter to a point on its tributary the Koktcha, beyond Faizábád. Speaking roughly, the territory may be divided into five distinct parts; to the north-east, is Kábulistán or Afghánistán proper, the country of which Kábul is the capital, between the Hindu Kush to its north and Ghazni and the Saféd Koh to its south, and from the Khaibar Pass to the Koh-i-Baba; to the north of that again, sloping to the Oxus and its tributary, is Badakshan, with its dependent district of Vakhan, from the Sarikul on the east to the junction of the Koktcha river with the Oxus, the latter forming the northern boundary of this

Afghán province through its entire extent; to the west of Badakshan, Afghán Turkistán, comprising the districts of Kunduz, Khulm, and Balkh; further westward still, the districts of Aksha, Seripul, Maimené, Shibberjan, and Andkhoi, the latter of which is the extreme Afghán frontier possession to the north-west; to the west and south-west, Khorásán or Zabulistán, comprising Herát, the land of the upper Múrgháb, Gúrdistán, the Hazáreh mountain lands, the lands watered by the Helmund and the desert of Sëistán. The natural boundary to the north is the magnificent range of the Hindu Kush, sloping northwards towards the Oxus, which, in a military sense, forms its ditch. Separated from the Hindu Kush by the famous Bamián Pass, but continuing its course westward, rises the ever snow-bearing Koh-i-Baba, spouting from its southern slopes the water which forms the Helmund, which runs a course of about four hundred miles to the south-west. To this lofty range are linked on likewise, to the westward, two parallel ranges, the Saféd Koh and the Siah-Koh, which embrace the valley of the Heri-rúd. The first of these is equally well known as the Paropamisan range. Between Herát and Kábul, running southwards as far as the Argandáb, a tributary of the Helmund, the lofty peaks and chains of the Siah-Koh, separated from each other by streams issuing from its southern slopes, form the unexplored country of the Hazáreh. To the east, running almost directly north and south, is the great Sulaimán range, almost at right angles with the Saféd Koh, which strikes off from it westward at a point below Kábul. This Sulaimán range, which reaches as far as Balúchistán, forms a natural boundary between India and Persia. The stony, barren nature of the country as the mountain slopes to the latter, affords a striking contrast to the richness and fertility of the valleys on the Peshawar side. It is through this range that the Kábul river, forcing its way, has formed the famous Khaibar Pass, the pass which forms the road of communication between Kábul and the Indian frontier. It offers likewise a mode of communication between Eastern Afghánistán and Sindh by means of the Gomal Pass. Between these two great ranges, the Sulaimán and the Paropamisan range, which almost inclose in a right angle the high lands of Afghánistán proper, there run in a diagonal direction, from the north-east to the south-west, several distinct mountain ranges, amongst which those which rise to the east of Kandahar are the most considerable. To these natural uprisings to the north-east, the depressions to the south-west form a complete contrast. Here, at a height of about 1,350 feet above the sea, is to be found the Hamun or Sëistan lake, from ten to thirty miles broad, and more than eighty miles long, surrounded by deserts, but showing many traces of former wealth and cultivation. Of the rivers, it may briefly be said that the largest, the Helmund, after running, as I have stated, a course of 400 miles, empties itself into the Sëistan lake, which receives also the waters of the Adraskan from the north, and of the Farrah-rud from the east. The principal contributaries of the Helmund are, the Argándáb, which rises in one of the ranges between Kábul and Kandahar, and flows in a south-westerly direction, and the Dori. The Kábul river pierces the mountains between Jellalabad and Peshάwar to increase the waters of the Indus.

The climate partakes the character of the country. The extreme cold of the high ranges runs parallel with the extreme heat of the valleys. There prevails in many parts likewise a medium climate, extremely pleasant, and very much resembling that of the highlands of South Africa. The country is rich in natural products. Iron and lead abound in all the mountain ranges, especially in the slopes which enclose the valley of the Heri-rud : there, too, are to be found in abundance the willow, the poplar, the olive, maize, rice, saltpetre, and every variety of fruit. The fertility of that valley has caused the city which is its emporium to be styled the granary and garden of Central Asia. "We ascended," wrote Arthur Conolly from Herát, in 1831, "by one hundred and forty steps to the top of the highest minaret, and thence looked down upon the city, and the rich gardens and vineyards round and beyond it—a scene so varied and beautiful that I can imagine nothing like it, except, perhaps, in Italy." But, though the valley of the Heri-rud is the most fertile, it is not the only spot in Afghanistan favoured by nature. Vegetable products abound everywhere. Apples, apricots, figs, plums, and grapes are plentiful all over the country. The tobacco of Kandahar is famous. In the slopes in its vicinity coal, and more recently gold, have been discovered. Hemp, cotton, rhubarb, the castor-oil plant, orange trees, citrons, maize, roses, tulips, are likewise abundant.

To this brief outline of the country and its productions I must add a few lines regarding its people. The Afgháns, in this respect resembling the children of Israel, from whom they claim, though it is considered without sufficient reason, direct descent, are an aggregation of many distinct tribes, each of which possesses its own chief. Western Afghánistán is the headquarters of the Duranis—to which the family of the reigning Amír belongs—and the Ghilzais, the most numerous of all the tribes. To the east are the Berduranis, counting amongst them the Yussufzais, who have come mostly in contact with the British. Between these two principal divisions are smaller tribes, each with its own laws and its own characteristics. It is calculated that whilst the population of Kábulistán or Eastern

Afghánistán numbers 900,000; that of Sëistán 280,000; of Kimduz 400,00; of Khúlm 300,000; of Balkh and the city which has supplanted it, Takhtapúl, 64,000; of Andkhoi and Shibberjan 60,000; of Aksha 10,000; of Maimené 100,000; of Badakshan and Vakhan 300,000; that of the valley of the Heri-rud amounts to 1,170,000. It is worthy to be noted that the vast majority of these last are either pure Tadschicks (aboriginal inhabitants) or men of mixed Persian and Turki blood. But there are, likewise, the men of Hazáreh, numbering nearly 200,000, who are distinctly of Turanian origin; and the Kazilbáshis, pure Persians by descent, who number some 60,000. These constitute the Muhammadan population, and if we add to them 600,000 Hindus and Játs from India, who constistute the main industrial portion of the community, and a sprinkling of Armenians who belong to the same category, we shall obtain a very fair estimate of the actual number of the inhabitants.

The estimates regarding their character do not always agree. Mountstuart Elphinstone, whose insight into Asiatic character was remarkable, was probably right when he pronounced the Afghán to be a lover of liberty, brave, devoted to his family, true to his friends, but envious, avaricious, obstinate, and merciless. The best of all the tribes are the Duranis and Ghilzais. Originally shepherds, pasturing vast flocks in their native hills and valleys, these have preserved to a great extent their patriarchal customs. But however calm and stolid they may be ordinarily, it is a fact that they too, when roused, display to the full the worst qualities of the national character.

Of all the provinces acknowledging the rule of the Amir of Kábul Herát is the richest and most fertile. Important as is the part which it has already played in Central-Asian history, the future which is before it is more important still. In this year, or in the years immediately following this year, the city of Herát will be constituted either the strong barrier which will stop the approach of Russia towards India; or it will become the gate through which the Russian army, preceded by hordes of Turkoman cavalry, will attempt to follow in the steps of Alexander the Great, of Chengiz Khán, of Taimúr, of Nadir Sháh, and of Ahmad Sháh. To Herát, then, I propose to devote a separate chapter.

CHAPTER II.

HERÁT, OR THE FRONTIER OF AFGHÁNISTÁN COVERING THE APPROACH TO BRITISH INDIA.

THE Khanate of which the city of Herát is the capital, formed from west to east like a wedge, stretches from the slopes of the Paropamisan range to the marshy lake of Sëistan; on the west it is bounded by Persian Khorásán; on the east and south-east by the province of Kandahar and the Siah-koh. Between the spurs of that mountain and of the Paropamisus, and even more to the north, the Heri-rúd, which flows first westward and takes afterwards a northerly direction, waters a tableland which, fertile beyond fertility even as it is known in the East, constitutes an oasis surrounded by stony ridges, sandy wastes and by steppes. This favoured district covers an area of 120,000 square miles, and supports nearly a million and a half of inhabitants. In the northern portion dwell the Kazilbashis, Shiahs in religion and Persian in origin; the Aimaks, Súnis in faith and the descendants of the Iranian Tadschicks; and the Hazárehs, a Turanian race, speaking the Turki language and Shiahs by religion. More to the south the people are almost all Tadshicks, with a sprinkling of Afgháns, of Turkomans, and of Hindús.

The city which gives its name to this fertile region lies

four miles north of a point of the Heri-rúd, where that river is spanned by a bridge with twenty-six arches. It is about 420 miles to the west of the Afghán capital, Kábul, about 200 south-east of Meshed, and 202 miles south-east by south of Sarakhs. It forms a kind of irregular parallelogram surrounded by a thick mud wall from twelve to eighteen feet high, backed by a brick wall ten feet high and provided with thirty towers and five well-fortified gates. Herát has greatly fallen from the high position it held when it was described as the Pearl of the World.* The ruins in its vicinity testify to its former greatness. From that position it fell, partly perhaps in consequence of the rivalry of Meshed, supported by the wealth and influence of Persia, but mainly because of the constant wars and the long-continued oppression which in the course of a hundred and fifty years have caused the decrease of the population from a hundred thousand to a little more than one third of that number. Herát, however, the capital of the fertile oasis which covers the approaches to India, the centre point for the caravan routes of Central Asia, must ere long resume her lost position. Again will she become, whether under English auspices or under the auspices of Russia, the granary and garden of Central Asia. The crucial moment has now arrived to decide whether her splendid resources will be used for the invasion of India by Russia, or for the defence of India against that aggressive power.

A glance at the past history of Herát with be sufficient to prove the vital importance of this question. The Mogol rulers who preceded the British in the occupation of India always recognised the necessity of guarding in their own

* "Khorásán is the oyster-shell of the world, and Herát is its Pearl."—*Eastern Proverb.*

hands the key of that portal. When in the decay of their empire they lost that key, two invasions from the north speedily followed. The invaders destroyed and retired, but the destruction they effected so weakened the Mogol dynasty that it fell an easy prey to the first invader from beyond the seas.

But it was not the Mogols alone who recognized the importance of Herát as the outlying bulwark of India. With one solitary exception, that of Báber—to be presently noticed—every invader from the north has deemed the conquest of Herát as the first necessary preliminary to an attack upon India. So thought Alexander the Great (327 B.C.); so thought Chengiz Khán (1219–22 A.D.); so thought Taimur (1381 A.D.). In the time of Báber indeed Herát was the shuttlecock between the Persians and the Uzbeks, and Báber, who possessed Kábul, solved the question whilst they were fighting by cutting into the Herát line at Kandahar (1525–26 A.D.). At a later period, 1731, the conqueror of Persia, the Khorasáni Nadir Sháh, did not dare to dream even of the conquest of India until he had conquered both Herát and Kandahar. He did not grudge the four months which he found necessary to take the first, nor the thirteen required to subdue the opposition of the second. His successor in the career of conquest, Ahmad Sháh, a Durani Afghán, followed the same lines (1747–61); and, by his success, crushed the vitality out of the ruling dynasty of India. An Afghán, cherishing the snow-clad hills of his native country, he conquered, plundered, and retired. Under similiar circumstances, a European invader, who to gain a similar result should have traversed sandy deserts and crossed rocky steppes, would conquer—and remain!

The conquest of Délhi by Ahmad Sháh, May 1757; his

second occupation of the Imperial city the year following and the crowning victory of Pánipat (January 1761) dealt the reigning dynasty of India a blow under which it reeled and from which it never recovered. The very same year which saw the first conquest of Dihli witnessed likewise, on the plain of Plassey, a victory which planted the British firmly in Bengal. Whilst Ahmad Sháh retired, satiated with slaughter and with plunder, the British remained and pushed forward. The edifice of Mogol dominion was rotten to the core. It fell, less from the efforts of the British than from the decay which had sapped its foundations. Until 1857-8 India had never, in the true sense of the term, been conquered by the British. The natives of India who preferred the rule of law to the rule of anarchy and spoliation, had fought under the British banner for the principles which secured to them the possession of their own lands, the safety of their wives and children. Fighting on these lines,—the fight almost invariably forced upon them—the British advanced steadily till they reached the frontier line of the Sutlej. The country beyond that frontier line, the country of the Five Rivers, the Panjáb, was ruled at the time by one of the most astute sovereigns who has ever sat upon an eastern throne. But in 1836-7 Ranjit Singh was growing old. In the mountainous country beyond his northern frontier Dost Muhammad, a young ruler of the Baruckzye clan of the Duráni tribe, was rising into notice in the eastern world. Herát, which had not been heard of since Ahmad Sháh had sacked it, on the death of Nadir Sháh, in 1749, but which during the long period had been declining under the misrule and oppression of its foreign masters, came once more to be talked about. A Persian army, it was rumoured throughout the bazaars of India and Central Asia, was marching against the capital of the fertile country watered by the Heri-rúd, and with that army, controlling its movements and instructing its soldiers, marched likewise many Russian officers and some hundreds of Russian soldiers. The rumour spreading onwards reached the Governor-General of India in Calcutta: it was passed on to the Secretary for Foreign Affairs in London. That minister recognized at a glance all its significance, all its importance. The name of that minister was Lord Palmerston!

CHAPTER III.

THE FIRST CONNECTION BETWEEN ENGLAND AND HERÁT.

THE keen vision of Lord Palmerston had detected, I have said, at a glance, all the significance, all the importance of the news that a Persian army, guided and controlled by Russian officers, was marching on Herát ; he had recognized that, should that march be successful, Herát would become a Persian Herát controlled by Russia. The armed intrigue must be met and baffled at all hazards.

The issues which were so quickly discerned by Lord Palmerston in London were not, unfortunately, so clear to the vision of the Governor-General of India and his Council. The most obvious method to accomplish the desired end would have been to lend efficient support to the ruler of Afghánistán. It was certain that Dost Muhammad desired as little as Lord Palmerston the occupation of the second city of his dominions by a Russo-Persian army.

That there existed difficulties in the way of a course so pointed is true. The greatest of these difficulties lay in the fact that whilst Dost Muhammad exercised supreme authority in Kábulistán, or easterm Afghánistán, his influence in Kandahar and Herát was little more than nominal. In the former his brothers held sway, and his brothers, jealous of his authority, were very much disposed to accept the Sháh of Persia as their suzerain : they had even made advances to Russia.

In Herát the position was still less favourable. There ruled Prince Kámran, son of the ex-Sháh of Afghánistán, Mahmud Sháh, a monster of wickedness and debauchery, virtually as an independent prince. He, too, disliked the idea of being conquered by Persia; but he hated still more the prospect of being relieved by Dost Muhammad, for he had murdered the eldest brother of that chief, and efficient aid from such a source would mean death to himself.

Such, then, was the position, as it presented itself in 1837, to the Governor-General of India, Lord Auckland, and his advisers. It must be admitted that is was beset with difficulties; for efficient aid to the ruler of Kábul, an aid sufficient to enable him to march to the relief of Herát, would throw at once that city into the hands of Persia. For it was clear that Prince Kámran would make terms with the Persians rather than submit to Dost Muhammad.

Lord Auckland despatched at that time an embassy to Dost Muhammad, on, what was termed, a commercial mission. The chief member of this embassy was Captain Alexander Burnes, an officer of the Bombay army, possessing rare ability, a colloquial knowledge of the languages of Central Asia, and a thorough acquaintance, acquired by travelling alone dressed as a native in the countries beyond the Oxus, with the habits and modes of thought of the children of the soil. Burnes reached Kábul the 20th of September, 1837, and was extremely well received by the Amír. He found him, however, more intent upon the recovery of Pesháwar, which had been filched from him some years before by Ranjit Singh, than on the recovery of Herát. Burnes, whilst holding out to him no hope that his views would be regarded with favour, forwarded reports of his interviews with the Amír to the Governor-General. Before he could receive a reply another agent appeared upon the field.

This new agent was a young Russian officer named Viktevich. Viktevich was a Lithuanian, who, exiled for his share in a Polish Conspiracy, had spent his time in travel in Central Asia, had gained the pardon of his Government, and who was now employed to undertake a secret mission to Kábul. The object of his mission was to counteract and render nugatory the influence of Burnes.

At the first it appeared as though the young Lithuanian would fail. Dost Muhammad, still hopeful of a favourable reply from India, scarcely noticed him. But when, on the 21st February, a reply came from the Governor-General intimating courteously but plainly, that whilst he was ready to treat with the Amír on matters affecting the Persian expedition, he would not aid him to recover Pesháwar, he changed his tone. Turning to the Russian agent, the Amír obtained from him all the promises he desired. In return Viktevich obtained his sanction to conclude an alliance between the Kandahar brothers of the Amír and Persia.

On the 26th April, Burnes, utterly hopeless of success, turned his back on Kábul. The failure of his endeavour to make a friend and ally of the then *de facto* ruler of Afghánistán made Lord Palmerston resolve to supplant him by a sovereign who should be nothing else in his foreign policy than a tool and agent of the British. Under his instructions, then, Lord Auckland brought a royal member of the family of Sháh Ahmad, the ex-king Sháh Shuja, from his enforced exile at Ludiáná, and directed the assembly of a considerable army to replace him on the throne of Kábul.

But before the army could be fully assembled, the object which Lord Palmerston had most at heart had been accomplished in an unforeseen and unexpected manner. A young Englishman, Eldred Pottinger, had entered the Bombay Artillery in the year 1827. Active, industrious, eager to gain knowledge and quick in acquiring it, young Pottinger had early obtained a political staff appointment in Sindh under his uncle, Colonel, afterwards Sir Henry, Pottinger. Anxious to explore the countries and to make himself acquainted with the habits and manners of the people between the Indus and the Oxus and beyond the latter river, Eldred obtained, in 1837, his uncle's permission to visit those lands as an independent traveller. Disguising himself as a horsedealer from Kachh, young Pottinger crossed the Indus and, travelling in a manner the least likely to attract attention, took the road to Kábul. From that capital he resolved to proceed to Herát, but, aware that in the disguise of a saintly character his nationality would be still less likely to be discovered, he threw off the garb of a horsedealer and assumed that of a Saiad or Holy man. After many adventures, including a dangerous detention by a Hazáreh chief which promised at one time to put a forcible end to his wanderings, Pottinger reached Herát in safety. This was on the 18th August. He was still there when, a month later, information reached the city that a Persian army was marching against it. On the arrival of this news the ruler, Prince Kámran, was at his wits' end. His prime minister and factotum, Yár Muhammad, showed, however, a resolution worthy of the occasion. Not only did he announce his determination to defend the city to the last, but he took all the means of which he was master to strengthen its defences and to increase the garrison.

Never was a danger more real. The Russian minister at Teheran, Count Simonitch, had not only advanced fifty thousand tomaunns to the Sháh, but had promised that potentate that if he would take Herát the balance of the debt due by Persia to Russia should be remitted. He went even further. He gave him, to aid in the attack, a

Russian general, General Barofski; encouraged him to employ General Samson, a Russian in the Persian service; and, with that general, two thousand Russian soldiers who, to save appearances, were officially described as deserters from the Russian army!

Upon Eldred Pottinger the information that a Persian army so commanded and so assisted was advancing against Herát produced an electric effect. A British officer, possessing skill, energy, daring, and that self-reliant character the display of which by the sons of Great Britain has made the British empire, he felt that the time for disguise had passed, that he must avow himself and take his part in the defence of the threatened city. He did avow himself to the minister, was well received, was presented to Prince Kámran, and was authorized by both to assist in the defence.

The siege began the 22nd November following. It lasted more than nine months—till the 8th of September, 1838. Of that siege Eldred Pottinger, the only Englishman within the walls of the city, was the hero. True it was that the earthwork defences were crumbling and in disrepair: true, that the parapets were so rotten that they fell like timber before the fire of the light guns of the besiegers: true, that the Russian allies of the Persians, furnished with the modern appliances of Europe, inspired the garrison with the fear that they were mining under the walls. This was all true, but the indomitable Englishman was present ever to repair breaches, to lead a rallying party, to meet mine with countermine. During the siege he, at the request of Prince Kámran, visited the Persian camp with proposals for accommodation. These, however, were refused, and the attack recommenced more furiously than before. But the steadfast purpose of the garrison was not to be shaken: they repaired every breach and repulsed every assault. On the 19th April, Major D'Arcy Todd, an officer of the Bengal Artillery, who had been for many years employed in the Persian army and had won the respect of all with whom he had come in contact, entered the city, under a flag of truce, with a message from the Sháh. He was the first Englishman who had ever appeared in Herát wearing a British uniform, and his tight-fitting clothes, contrasting with the loose garments of the Asiatics, roused the most vivid curiosity. Major Todd came to announce that the Sháh was ready to accept British mediation. He returned with the message that Prince Kámran was equally agreeable to such a course. Not for a moment, however, did hostilities cease in consequence of that agreement. The siege was conducted as vigorously as before. Shortly afterwards, however, the Sháh withdrew from his offer to accept the arbitration of the British.

Month followed month, and the Russo-Persian army still plied the city with shot and shell. Every day, however, brought fresh misery to the besieged. Food became very scarce; the stench caused by the want of sewers or any means of drainage almost unendurable; in the month of May famine and pestilence stalked hand in hand through the streets. Under the influence of these dread twin-sisters the defence began to flag, and the breaches remained unrepaired. Everything presaged an early and fatal termination of the siege.

It is under such circumstances that a great man is really divine. It is not too much to say that at this conjuncture Eldred Pottinger became, in the eyes of the Herátis, the object of their trust, their veneration, their every hope. He was to them what Gordon was in 1884 to the people of Khartoum. These feelings were specially manifested on the 24th June. On that day the besiegers made a well-planned and very determined attack on four parts of the city. At three of these they were repulsed. But at the fourth, they had almost carried the breach when the Vizier, Yár Muhammed, accompanied by Pottinger reached the spot. Yár Muhammed was a brave man, but he was cowed by the sight which met his gaze—the sight of the garrison giving way before their advancing foe. He urged them to rally, but he was too overcome himself to give them the example. Then was Pottinger's opportunity. He made a despairing appeal to the Vizïer, inspired him with a portion of his own resolution; then, with his aid, he re-formed the now encouraged defenders and forced back the foe.

The month of July passed without any renewal of activity on the part of the besiegers. On the 11th of the following month the Sháh received in his camp an English officer, Colonel Stoddart, deputed to inform him that the continuance of the siege meant war with England. Little less than one month later the Persian army retired behind its own frontier!

The conclusion that, because the Persians after a siege of ten months' duration were in the end repelled, Herát was therefore impregnable, would be entirely fallacious. Eldred Pottinger deliberately declared that Muhammed Sháh might have taken the city by assault within twenty-four hours after his appearance before its walls if his troops had been efficiently commanded. We may go further and add—to use the language of the historian of the events of that period—the late Sir John Kaye—that but for the heroism of the young Bombay Artilleryman, Herát would under the actual circumstances have fallen!

With the raising of the siege of Herát the necessity for English intervention in the affairs of Afghánistán had disappeared. The object originally contemplated by Lord

Palmerston had been accomplished. Russia had received a check in her endeavour to use Persia as a cat's paw to filch away the most important of all the positions covering India. If England, on the retirement of the Persian army, had entered into an arrangement with Dost Muhammad, an arrangement for which he was then eager, the relations between India and the mountainous country which is naturally its frontier redoubt, would have been settled on a firm basis. But, unfortunately, before the raising of the siege of Herát had become known, Lord Auckland had pledged himself to Sháh Shuja, and it was determined to carry out the policy of substituting for a ruler of doubtful fidelity a prince who in all his foreign relations would be the tool of England.

It is not necessary here to do more than record the failure of that unfortunate policy. After nearly four years of desperate venture, it resulted in the restoration to supreme sway in Kábul of the prince whom we had expelled.

Embittered as he naturally was against the people who had expelled him, Dost Muhammad returned to Kábul with a far higher idea of the resources of the British nation than he had held before his enforced exile. He had visited Calcutta and seen their ships, their arsenals, their fortresses, and, though many years elapsed before he entered into friendly relations with his old enemies, he was resolved from the first moment of his return to do nothing to tempt them to renew their attack upon himself. It is true that in the death-throes of the struggle for the Panjáb, he allowed one of his sons to lead a cavalry brigade to assist the Sikhs in the battle which consummated their overthrow; but after the British frontier had been permanently advanced beyond the Indus, he remained for a time quiescent. The renewed intrigues of Persia for the recovery of Herát forced him at last to renew friendly relations with his old enemy.

In that year, 1854, his son Ghulam Haidar visited Pesháwar for that purpose. He was met there by the late Lord Lawrence, at the time plain John Lawrence, Chief Commissioner of the Panjáb. On that occasion the famous agreement was signed in which the Amir of Afghánistán covenanted "to be the friend of the friends, and the enemy of the enemies of the Honble. East India Company."

If we reflect for a moment upon this most important agreement, we shall arrive at the inevitable conclusion that it accomplished little more than the carrying of political relations back to the point at which they were when Burnes visited Kábul in 1837–8. It blotted out the intervening events. The first Afghán war had, in a word, lost for us eighteen years which might have well been employed in cementing relations necessary for the safety of the British empire in India.

Doubtless the political aspect which prompted the Amír to send his son to Pesháwar, had many points of similarity with the political aspect of 1837. On both occasions Herát was threatened by the same Asiatic power, stirred up by the same European power. But if the English had grown wiser, so likewise had Dost Muhammad. He no longer talked of recovering Pesháwar. He saw the full significance of the movement about Herát, and he wanted the support of the English to baffle it.

In 1854 England was at war with Russia; that power therefore, only exercised a legitimate right when, the barriers of an independent Caucasus still existing, she incited Persia to renew her attempts upon the fortified city which had repulsed her in 1838.

The incitations of Russia produced corresponding action on the part of Persia. She sent an army in the autumn of 1856 against Herát, and that city, no longer defended by an Eldred Pottinger, surrendered to her in the month of October of the same year.

But Lord Palmerston was Prime Minister of England; and Lord Palmerston was firmly resolved that Persia should not hold the city, and with the city the province which would constitute a new base for an army hostile to British India. Herát had, I have said, fallen in October 1856. On the 1st November, Lord Palmerston declared war against Persia, and despatched an army to attack her on her most vulnerable side, in the Persian gulf.

Never has an expedition been better planned or better executed. Never certainly has energetic action obtained more promptly the desired result. War was declared, I have said, the 1st November, 1856. Peace was signed the 4th March, 1857. In the interval, Persia had been defeated in two battles. By the terms of the peace she agreed to restore Herát to the Afgháns!

Before the signature of the Peace, the British acting by the mouth of Mr. John Lawrence, had signed another agreement with the Amír promising him a monthly allow- of £10,000 and arranging for the permanent residence of a British agent—a native of India—at Kábul. In the course of the years immediately following, Dost Muhammad brought Western Afghánistán, including Herát, more completely under his own personal sway.

On his death, in 1863, a civil war ensued for the succession. That war lasted, with varying fortunes, for five years. It was only in January 1869, that the most capable of the sons of Dost Muhammad, Sher Ali, obtained over his last remaining rival, the present Amír Abdul Rahman, a victory so crushing that from that moment all opposition ceased, and Afghánistán with its borders as they are described in the first two pages of the first chapter became united under one head.

CHAPTER IV.

THE PROGRESS OF RUSSIA TOWARDS INDIA.

In 1854 Nicholas, Czar of all the Russias, struck his long meditated blow for the possession of Constantinople. He failed, and he died. His successor, Alexander II., made peace with the two great western powers who had baffled his father, and announced ostentatiously that it was his intention to devote himself to domestic reforms. As an earnest of his sincerity he abolished serfdom.

But whilst hoodwinked Europe was praising the sagacity, the prudence, and the moderation of the young Czar, that astute prince was straining his empire to break down the mountain barrier which barred his free access to the steppes of Central Asia. The very year that witnessed the signature of the Peace of Paris (April 1856) saw him hurl an army of 150,000 men against the passes of the Caucasus. Fiercely did the heroic mountaineers resist. But numbers prevailed. At the end of three years the strongholds of the Caucasus had been stormed; the hero who had led the resistance, the illustrious Schamyl, was a prisoner (6 September 1859), and the mountaineers, who had for so many years successfully defied Russia, had abandoned their native fastnesses to seek refuge within the dominions of the Sultan.

The Caucasus conquered, Russia, who for some years had been working her way across the low undulating plains which lie between the Alatan range and the Jaxartes, made her spring across that river. The Khanate of Khokand, having a population of three millions, was the first object of her attack. For the moment she spared it to effect the capture of the city of Tchemkend. This capture brought her into collision with the troops of Bokhára—a collision which resulted in the defeat of the Amír of that place and the occupation of the town of Turkistan, two hundred and twenty miles from Khokand.

To allay the apprehensions of England the Russian Prime Minister, Prince Gortschakoff, proceeded (November, 1864) to issue a kind of manifesto. In this remarkable document the Prince justified the permanent occupation of the two towns I have mentioned, on the plea that hostilities against them had been rendered necessary by the predatory instincts of the populations bordering the Russian frontier. He proceeded, then, to imply, though he was careful not to state absolutely, that the final point of Russian advance had been reached. "Russia," he declared, "was now in the presence of a more solid and compact, less unsettled and better organized social state; fixing for us with geographical precision the limit up to which we must advance, and at which we must halt."

The ink with which this manifesto was penned was barely dry, when Russia deliberately departed from the pacific programme which it sketched out. Under the pretence that some of her officers whom she had dispatched to Bokhára to negotiate, had been unduly detained in that city, she renewed her hostilities with the Amír. Tashkend, an important town in the valley of the Chirchik, with a population of 80,000 souls, the great emporium of Central Asia for cotton and rice, some ninety miles from Khokand, fell before her troops (June 1865). But no sooner was she assured of this conquest than she again appeared before Europe with protestations and excuses. Again did she declare (September 1865) by the voice and despatches of the Prime Minister, that the Czar "had no desire to add further to his dominions." Scarcely, again, was the ink of the despatch dry, when (1866) the troops of the Czar made a spring upon and captured the walled town of Khojend, the key of the Jaxartes, seventy miles from Khokand, like Tashkend, a great manufactory of cotton goods, and possessing a population of 20,000. Before Europe could learn even of this new conquest Russian troops had overrun the province of Khokand, known also as Ferghana. By a ukase dated July 1867 the Czar formally annexed one half of this rich and fertile province with an area of more than 28,000 square miles to the Russian empire. The remaining half he conferred for the moment, and only for the moment, upon a native chieftain, to be held under the suzerainty of the Russian crown.

The time had now arrived when Russia conceived it necessary to make a still more important step. Bokhára had been snubbed and humiliated, but in the minds of the populations of Central Asia the influence of the powerful Amír of that independent state was still preponderant. It was necessary to cause that influence visibly to diminish. It is always easy to pick a quarrel. General Kaufman, the new military commander in Central Asia, proceeded then to establish a fortified post in dangerous contiguity to the famous city of Samarkhand, a hundred and thirty miles to the east of the capital. The insult was resented and war ensued. To a war between forces so unequally matched there could be but one result. Russia occupied and annexed Samarkhand. It was the most important conquest she had till then achieved. Its immediate result was to force the most venerated chief of Central Asia, the Amír of Bokhára, to become a tributary of the Czar!

These events happened in 1868. I was in India at the time, and I can well recollect the profound impression which the capture and annexation of the famous city of Samarkhand produced in the bazaars of that country. The fame of Samarkhand had spread over all Asia. In the imaginations of it's several populations it was the second city of the world, scarcely inferior, if at all inferior, to the Rúm—the Constantinople—of the Caliph of the Muhammadan faith. And now Samarkhand had fallen! What wonder if the mind of the untravelled Oriental could scarcely grasp the greatness of the people who had captured it!

The reader will do well to bear in mind that the annexation of Samarkhand was almost synchronous with the termination of the five years' civil war in Afghánistán. During that civil war the relations between India and its mountainous borderland had not improved. For whilst the Viceroy of India, Sir John Lawrence, had endeavoured to maintain a rigid impartiality between the contending rivals, the victor, Sher Ali, loudly complained of the little friendliness which had been displayed towards himself. Whilst then the year which witnessed Sher Ali sole ruler of Afghánistán found the relations between that country and British India extremely strained, it saw Russia planted on the eastern Oxus and its tributaries, within striking distance of the north-eastern portion of the dominions of the ruler of Kábul.

It would appear that this near approach of Russia attracted the attention of the British Government. Forgetting that Russia is really an Asiatic power, and that those who deal with her in diplomacy should always bear in mind that deception, or excellence in the art of deceiving, is regarded as the chiefest virtue in an Asiatic politician, Lord Clarendon, early in 1869, suggested to Prince

Gortschakoff the desirability of constituting Afghánistán a neutral zone. The astute Chancellor of the Russian empire caught the idea with enthusiasm. He hastened to declare that his master the Czar, "*looks upon Afghánistán as completely outside the sphere within which Russia may be called upon to exercise her influence.*" Meanwhile, however, the Government of India had objected, and very properly objected, to Lord Clarendon's proposal. Afghánistán, said the Governor-General in so many words, can never be a neutral zone for India: it is bound to India geographically and politically, and must continue so to be bound. And in that light it is necessary that Afghánistán should be regarded by Russia!

Upon this question the negociations with Russia were prolonged for two years, the Russian Government continuing to protest throughout that period that "Russia had no further intention of going south" and that "extension of territory was extension of weakness." Ultimately it was decided by the two Powers that the boundary of Afghánistán should be fixed, and it was agreed that all the countries in the effective possession of Sher Ali, and those which had previously acknowledged the rule of Dost Muhammad, should be comprised within that boundary. It was further arranged that the memoranda and papers on this subject should be submitted to General Kaufman, as the person nearest the spot capable of judging the question, in order that he might report to the Russian Government what were the actual boundaries. The matter drifted on. General Kaufman sent no report. Finally, on October, 17, 1872, Lord Granville wrote a dispatch to Lord Augustus Loftus, for communication to the Russian Government, in which he stated that the British Government, not having received any information from Russia, had been obliged to define the frontier in the mode they considered most just. Lord Granville then marked out the several lines of demarcation as I have stated them in the first chapter. This frontier was accepted by Russia, and the acceptance notified by Prince Gortschakoff in dispatches dated the 7th (19th) December, 1872, and the 19th (31st) January, 1873. Meanwhile Russia had been pertinaceously maturing the plans which she had long nursed with respect to Khiva. To enable the reader to understand this subject thoroughly I must digress for a moment from the continuous course of the story.

Even so far back as the time of Peter the Great, Khiva had been an object of Russian greed. The disastrous fate however, which attended an expedition, despatched in 1716 by that famous monarch had for long acted as a deterrent. Three attempts to explore were subsequently made, prior to the ascension of the Emperor Paul; the first by a simple agent in 1731; the second by a surveyor ten years later; and the third by an oculist favoured by the Empress Catherine, named Blankenagal, in 1793. Blankenagal on his return wrote a narrative of his travels, in which he painted in terms so glowing the wealth of Khiva and its importance as a commercial centre that it inflamed the Emperor Paul, —who though murdered because his murderers called him mad, had ever a method in his madness—to re-open the idea so long held in abeyance. He actually despatched Count Orloff at the head of a considerable force in 1801 to carry out his views. Orloff had reached Irgiz, now known as Fort Uralsk, when he heard of the assassination of his master. He returned, and during the vast European complications which followed the accession of Alexander I., the subject was laid on the shelf. It was taken up again in 1819, when Captain Mouravieff was despatched from the army of the Caucasus to reconnoitre the eastern shores of the Caspian, to select there a spot for the erection of a fort, and to proceed thence to Khiva. Escorted by a few friendly Turkomans Mouravieff reached Khiva in safety. There, however, he was seized by order of the Khán, imprisoned, and detained for nearly seven weeks before he was allowed to return. It would seem that his presence in Khiva excited the strong suspicions of the Khán and his advisers, for, subsequently to his return, the Turkomans of the desert inaugurated a system of pillage with respect to the Russian caravans such as they had never dreamt of before. Possibly their action was stimulated by the unwonted appearance of Russian soldiers at various points in the steppe, avowedly with the purpose of affording protection to their trading countrymen. There is little reason to doubt that even these nomads suspected that armed parties who occupied military forts on the steppe, nominally to protect Russian caravans, might gradually take root there, and even advance further.

The system of plunder inaugurated by the Khivans became at last so unbearable that, in 1839, General Perovski was despatched from Orenburg, with 5,235 men and twenty-two guns, to punish the Khán. The intense cold of the winter, the difficulties and inhospitalities of the steppe, fought hard, however, for Khiva. After losing one third of his force before accomplishing half the distance between Orenburg and the threatened city, Perovski was compelled to retrace his steps. The sufferings of his force during the retreat were extreme.

With the exception of the despatch of two minor missions in 1841 and 1842, both abortive in their results, no further serious move with respect to Khiva was made by Russia for nineteen years. In the meanwhile however two English officers, one Captain (now General) James Abbott, who has written a most interesting account of his mission; the other, the late Sir Richmond Shakespeare, had penetrated to Khiva from Herát, and had persuaded the Khán to release the Russian prisoners still languishing in captivity. After that there followed the lull of nineteen years. But, in 1858, at the very time, be it remembered, when, after the Crimean war, the barrier of Caucasus was being assailed, General Ignatieff, subsequently the well-known ambassador at Constantinople, was despatched on a special mission to Khiva and Bokhára. The mission of Ignatieff was outwardly one merely of compliment, and it led to no result. It may in fact be pronounced a failure, for, notwithstanding his great persuasive powers, the astute Russian neither succeeded in persuading the Khán of Khiva to sign the treaty which he had prepared and brought with him, nor in inducing him to put a stop to the raid on the Russian caravans.

Russia determined at length to put a final stop to these outrages. In 1869 she completed a strong fort and naval station at Krasnovodsk on the Caspian. She supplemented these the year following by erecting another fort and another naval station at Tchikislar, the point where the Atrek flows into the sea. Able now to despatch expeditions from a new base resting on the Caspian, she prepared in 1871 and 1872 to take decisive action.

The rumour of these preparations reached the Khán of Khiva and frightened him not a little. As he still refused, however, to accept the terms offered by Russia, or to receive a Russian envoy in his capital, dreading them *et dona ferentes*, Russia resolved to strike the blow she had been preparing. In July 1872, then, she fitted out and despatched an expedition under the command of General Markazoff. That officer, setting out from Tchikislar, easily reached Igly, on the old bed of the Oxus, and just within the borders of the Kara Kúm desert. At this point began the natural difficulties of his route. The Turkomans came to augment them. These daring horsemen surrounded Markazoff, cut off his baggage camels, and finally forced him (September 1872) to an ignominious retreat.

Russia could not allow such a defeat to pass unavenged. She organised a new and more powerful expedition, and placed at the head of it the general whose conquest of Samarkhand had made him the best known European in Central Asia—the famous General Kaufman. At the same time, to still the apprehensions of England, already roused by the magnitude of the preparations, the Czar instructed his ambassador at the Court of St. James's to declare that though an expedition would be despatched, it would be "a very little one"; that it would consist of but four and a half battalions; and that its purpose was simply and solely to punish acts of brigandage. "*Far from it being the intention of the Czar,*" added the ambassador, "*to take possession of Khiva, positive orders had been issued to prevent it.*"

I pause here for a moment to call attention to this principle of Russian policy, now renewed on the borders of Afghánistán—the principle of protesting moderation at St. Petersburg whilst the agents on the spot are spurred on to action which shall be decisive. How that action works is well described in the following letter written by Lord Palmerston to Lord Clarendon, and which has recently been republished in the *Times*, March 23:—

"The policy and practice of the Russian Government has always been to push forward its encroachments as fast and as far as the apathy or want of firmness of other Governments would allow it to go, but always to stop and retire when it was met with decided resistance, and then to wait for the next favourable opportunity to make another spring on its intended victim. In furtherance of this policy, the Russian Government has always had two strings to its bow—moderate language and disinterested professions at St. Petersburg and at London; active aggression by its agents on the scene of operations. If the aggressions succeed locally, the St. Petersburg Government adopts them as a *fait accompli* which it did not intend, but cannot in honour recede from. If the local agents fail they are disavowed and recalled, and the language previously held is appealed to as a proof that the agents have overstepped their instructions. This was exemplified in the Treaty of Unkiar-Skelessi, and in the exploits of Simonivitch and Viktevitch in Persia. Orloff succeeded in extorting the Treaty of Unkiar-Skelessi from the Turks, and it was represented as a sudden thought, suggested by the circumstances of the time and place, and not the result of any previous instructions; but having been done, it could not be undone. On the other hand, Simonivitch and Viktevitch failed in getting possession of Herát, in consequence of our vigorous measures of resistance; and as they failed, and when they had failed, they were disavowed and recalled, and the language previously held at Petersburg was appealed to as a proof of the sincerity of the disavowal, although no human being with two ideas in his head could for a moment doubt that they had acted under specific instructions.—July 31, 1853." (*Vide* Lord Palmerston's Life, Vol. II., 273, 12mo. ed.)

I now return to the date whence I digressed to deal with the earlier dealings of Russia with Khiva to the close of the period of the two years which followed Lord Clarendon's unfortunate proposition that Afghánistán should be regarded as a neutral zone, and the reception of the reply of Russia that she looked upon Afghánistán as completely outside the sphere within which Russia might be called to exercise her influence. That lull of two years had been spent by Russia in preparing an expedition which should deal finally, "once and for ever," with Khiva. Reports from their agents at Persia and elsewhere that such an expedition was preparing had, during that period, reached the British Government, and that Government had instructed its ambassador at St. Petersburg to ascertain the exact state of the case. The Russian Chancellor always denied that any expedition was in preparation, and his words on this point were so forcible, so explicit, and so absolute that the British Ambassador could not but accept them. The scales, at last, fell from his eyes. Towards the close of 1872, Lord A. Loftus informed his Government that he had gained the conviction that such an expedition had been decided upon, and would take place as soon as weather and circumstances would permit. Still the Government of the Czar and the Russian Ambassador in London continued to evade and to deny. Forced at last to admit that there was to be an expedition, they pleaded pathetically that it was to be on a very small scale, that it would consist of but four and a half battalions, and that it was designed merely to punish acts of brigandage. Then followed the memorable declaration which I cited in a preceding paragraph, and which I here repeat—a declaration typical of the value which it is always necessary to place on the words of Russian Czars, Russian Chancellors, and Russian ambassadors; "*Far from it being the intention of the Czar to take possession of Khiva, positive orders have been issued to prevent it.*"

What followed? The echo of the words I have italicised had scarce died away, when—not a mere "four and a half battalions," but five columns, numbering upwards of 12,000 men in all, started under the command in chief of General Kaufman, severally from Orenburg, from Tchikishlar, from Alexandrovsky, from Kazala, and from Jazakh, to converge on, and assault, Khiva. Yet, so great still were the natural difficulties of the route that the bulk of this army was saved from destruction by the merest accident. The Tchikishlar column had to fall back from Igly—the extreme point reached by Markazoff in the previous expedition; two of the other columns, with one of which was Kaufman himself, united, only to find themselves, a few days later, in the heart of a sandy desert, without supplies, without transport, without water. In this extremity they were saved from annihilation by a son of the desert, a ragged Kirghiz who disclosed the vicinity of wells containing abundant supplies of the precious fluid. The difficulties of the two remaining columns were more easily surmountable. Directed by the senior officer, General Verevkin, they reached Khiva, and took the city by assault. The natural result followed. Russia imposed her suzerainty upon the Khán, and annexed the whole of the Khivan territory on the right bank of the Oxus!

The capture and practical annexation of Khiva secured to Russia possession of the central point in the curved line which threatened the frontier of India. The left of that line was covered on its front by the Oxus and its confluents, and was flanked by Samarkhand; its centre was at Khiva, communicating with the left by the Oxus, and threatening alike Merv and Sarakhs; the right, based on the Caspian, would naturally creep along the northern frontier of Persia, subdue the Turkomans of the desert, then halt at a place within striking distance of Merv and Sarakhs; until, having neutralized or made a vassal of Persia, she should pounce upon those salient places, and prepare for the final spring which should land her in Herát.*

* These are not prophecies after the event. In his work on Herat, published in January, 1880; in his speeches after his visit to India in 1880–1; and in two articles entitled "Russian Conquests in the East," published in the *Army and Navy Magazine* in 1882, the author did his utmost to warn his countrymen of the inevitable issue.

But, not even the capture of Khiva, effected in spite of the denials and solemn assurances of the Czar and his ministers, could either rouse the British Government to a sense of the actual danger of the position, or weaken its faith in the promises of Russian diplomacy. The Secretary of State for Foreign Affairs, Lord Granville, not only declined to examine "too minutely how far these arrangements"—the annexation of Khiva—"were in strict accordance with the assurances given in January by Count Schouvaloff," but, hopeful still, he again addressed the Russian Chancellor on the subject of the two Governments arriving at a clear and frank understanding regarding their respective positions in Central Asia. There is a sublime irony in the tone of the reply of Prince Gortschakoff to this confiding overture. Having obtained, first, by hoodwinking the British Government all that he required, or rather, all that for the moment he was able to obtain, in Central Asia; and having in the second place obtained the forgiveness of the British Government for the violation of his plighted faith—a forgiveness accompanied by the expression of a hope that no such violation would occur in the future—Prince Gortschakoff expressed, in reply, his "entire satisfaction" with the "just view Lord Granville had taken!"

The conquest of Khiva left Russia face to face with the Turkomans. These hardy sons of the desert, kinsmen of the Osmánli who all but conquered Europe—for it was the grandfather of Osmán who, in the reign of Chengiz Khán, emigrated with his tribe of Turkomans to Asia Minor from Northern Khorásán—lived a wild and predatory life on the desert bordering the northern frontier of Khorásán. Herdsmen, they were likewise slave-dealers, nor should the fact be attributed to them as a crime. To capture and sell slaves had been the custom of the desert from time immemorial, and the wild, uninstructed Turkoman was in that respect not one whit behind his more cultivated rival the Khorásáni of Persian Khorásán. The Turkomans had the reputation of being the most skilful, the boldest, the most dashing horsemen of Central Asia. Nor was their martial record at all a blank. The fathers' fathers of the Turkomans of the present day had responded to the call of Nadir Sháh and had led the way for Ahmad Sháh Duráni to India. They had been foremost alike on the field of Panipat and in the sack of Dihli. Sons of freedom, impatient of restraint, they had taken no root in the land which they had helped to conquer, but had ever returned to the illimitable spaces of that sandy desert, the soil of which few but they ever cared to tread!

With men such as these, Russia, after her conquest of Khiva (June 1872) had to deal. Her policy, as usual, was direct. No notions of sentiment or of mercy would allow it to deviate a single hair's breath from its absolutely straight course. That policy may be summed up in six words. It was simply "to conquer, that she might use." Realizing the enormous advantage which might accrue to her in the years that were to come by the employment as her vanguard of a whole nation of "the finest horsemen in Central Asia" she yet felt the necessity of first dominating their spirits, of curbing their fierce love of independence, of, in a certain sense, breaking their spirits by the display of remorseless cruelty; that accomplished, the desert warriors would obey the power which would thus have subdued them, as implicity as their fathers' fathers had obeyed the orders of Nadir Sháh!

Moralists may talk of the civilizing mission of Russia, of the advantage which must accrue to the world from the extension of her sway in Central Asia. They forget the great truth which every English politician ought to repeat to himself every day and all day, the truth that Russia herself is in all essentials an Asiatic power, and should be treated diplomatically as one is accustomed to treat diplomatically every avowed Asiatic power.

I must ask now the moralist and the diplomat to accompany me into the great desert after the absolute sub mission of Khiva had been secured. There was a tribe of Turkomans, called the Yomud Turkomans, inhabiting the Hazávat district. The Yomuds were a Nomad people, whose sole wealth consisted in their flocks and herds; they had no ready cash. It was impossible for them to raise money by the sale of their cattle or their corn, or even of the jewels and ornaments of their wives and daughters, for in the desert there were no purchasers. Now General Kaufman had been engaged during the campaign in no actual battle. Without a fight he could not obtain the coveted Cross of St. George. He looked, then, to the desert for victims, and fixed his eye upon the Yomuds. Having ascertained all particulars regarding them, he imposed upon them the payment within ten days of a fine in money which he knew they could not pay. Vainly did they offer their jewels, their flocks, and their herds. The money was wanted, and they had it not, nor could they obtain it. Then, to punish their default, Kaufman inundated their country with his troops, ordered his generals to destroy their settlement, and to confiscate their herds and their property. His orders were obeyed with a refinement of mercilessness such as has never been surpassed in the records of crime.* The reign of terror was inaugurated!

From that time the warfare of Russia with the desert tribes was intermittent. It was not, however, till 1879 that

No one will suspect Schuyler of aught but sympathy with Russia: yet it is from his pages, and from the confirmatory letters of MacGahan, that I have drawn these facts.

the colossal Power of the North judged that the time had arrived to make an attempt to establish a permanent settlement in Turkoman territory. The point they selected for this purpose was Kizil Arvat, a place above, but slightly to the east of the highest point of the frontier of Persia, and not far south of the borders of the Kara-Kúm The intention, plainly manifested, of thus establishing themselves permanently on their highway was not at all relished by the desert-born warriors. The chief of the tribe of Akal Tekkes, Nur Verdi Khán, who till that time had been disposed to reciprocate the friendly overtures of the Russians, at once took the alarm. No sooner did the leader of the Russian force, General Lomakin, attempted to arrange for a permanent occupation, than Nur Verdi assailed him at the head of all the warrior horsemen of his tribe. No details of this, the first struggle for the possession of the desert, ever reached the Europe which is outside of Russia. But this, at least, transpired: Lomakin was eventually besieged in his camp, and was so pressed there that he was forced to abandon his guns and retreat in disorder, pursued by crowds of horsemen to Krasnovodsk. He was even besieged there for several weeks!

Again could not Russia afford to allow this check to remain unavenged. In August 1878, she despatched a larger force from Tchikishlar under the orders of the same general. This time Lomakin reached Khojá Kala, a few miles to the south of Kizil Arvat, in safety. But there he was assailed by the same enemies led by the same daring warrior. He and his Russians were driven out of Khojá Kala and were literally chased back to Tchikishlar, from under the very guns of which place the pursuers carried off hundreds of his camels!

A third expedition then became necessary in 1879. General Lazareff, who had greatly distinguished himself in the campaign in Armenia against Mukhtar Pasha in the previous year, was selected to command it. With Lomakin as his second in command, Lazareff set out at the head of his force—a force greatly in excess of that which had started in 1877—from Tchikishlar on the 18th June. His plan was to inflict a severe defeat on, and to dominate the spirit of the Turkomans before attempting to make a settlement. But at Tchát-i-Atrak, about midway to Kizil Arvat along the Persian frontier, Lazareff sickened and died. Lomakin, who succeeded him, and who shared his views, pushed on then to Kizil Arvat, and thence beyond Bámi, to a point within six miles of Dengli Tepé, a square built fort occupied by the Turkomans with their whole available force. On the 9th of September Lomakin marched against that not very formidable place. After a desperate battle, which lasted all day, and in which up to 5 P.M. they had all the advantage, the Russians were repulsed, and fell back, beaten, baffled, and humiliated, to the Caspian! They were unable even to reach that base before December had well set in!

But beaten, baffled, and humilitated though she had thrice been on this line, Russia adhered to her purpose with a steadfastness and pertinacity characteristic of her whole policy. Russia never surrenders a firmly-rooted idea. In 1880 she made preparations, on a still larger scale than before, to renew the attack on the line between Akhal and Askabad. To command the new expedition she summoned the man who enjoyed the highest reputation in her army, a man who possessed a European reputation for dash and daring, the leader of her war party, the famous Skobeleff.

Skobeleff possessed advantages which had been denied to Lomakin. In the spring then of 1880, the Turkoman chief who had led his countrymen to victory after victory, who in the course of his brilliant career had defeated three nations, the Khivans, the Persians, and the Russians, the illustrious Nur Verdi Khán, had died. He had left no successor at all equal to himself. Whilst therefore, in 1880, the Russians, alike more numerous and more experienced in the warfare of the desert than in 1879, were led by the best general of whom their country could boast, the Turkomans had no leader who inspired them with the confidence which, in 1879, had gone far to enable them to repulse their foes.

The plan devised by Skobeleff proved that he had completely mastered all the intricacies of the task which had been committed to his hands. Joined by a small body of men who marched from Khiva to the western border of the Tekke oasis, he marched with a select division, of which those men formed a part, from the Attrek to the Akhal oasis at Bámi, about 180 miles from the Caspian and about 80 from the spot where the Turkomans had congregated, a fort called Geok Tepé, somewhat to the north of the scene of the disaster of the previous year. He then proceeded to fortify this post, covering it with intrenchments, with the idea of making it the base for a further advance. He made of it in fact what Wellington made of the lines of Torres Vedras. Within the lines thus formed Skobeleff proceeded to store provisions and supplies, turning a deaf ear to the solicitations of those who pressed him to avenge without further delay the defeat of his predecessor. These supplies came from the Volga, from the Caucasus, and from Persia, and were conveyed by camel trains from Krasnovodsk. Several months were employed by Skobeleff in these necessary preliminaries. <At length, in January 1881, he advanced, attacked the children of the desert in their intrenchments at Geok Tepé, stormed their position, slaughtered thousands of the defenders, and pursued the remainder beyond Askabad. This time the rule of terror

did its work. It cowed the survivors into absolute and complete submission.

The usual political consequences followed. In the month of May of the same year the Czar issued an ukase by which he declared that the Transcaspian territory, the abode of the Akhal Tekkes, was annexed to Russia.

Nor was Russia worse served by her administrators than by her generals. In an incredibly short space of time, lines of rails, intended during the Russo-Turkish war for the use of the army of the Danube, and which had since been lying idle in Southern Russia, were transported to the eastern shore of the Caspian and were at once utilized in the newly acquired territories. So thoroughly in earnest were the officials, that before the conclusion of 1881 the line had been completed as far as Kizil Arvat, 144 miles from the Caspian. It is a remarkable fact, worthy of appreciation, that at that very moment the British Indian Government were selling the rails which had been brought at considerable expense to Quetta for the purpose of connecting Sibi with that important frontier fort, and that fort with Kandahar!

In a lecture of remarkable clearness and ability delivered at the Royal United Service Institution on the 16th May, 1884, Sir Edward Hamley, after describing the progress of Russia in the Transcaspian regions up to the period of Skobeleff's success at Geok Tepé in 1881, proceeded to point out how the Russians, never losing sight of the definite aim of their policy, had, whilst passing on the railway from the eastern shores of the Caspian to Kizil Arvat and beyond Kizil Arvat, been at the same time careful to unite to the empire by the same iron band the Caucasian shores of the same. After pointing out the advantages of Baku on the Caucasian shore, as producing an inexhaustible quantity of fuel for railway consumption, and informing his audience that at the end of 1882 the railway of the Caucasus was continued from Tiflis to Baku, with a branch to Batoum, a more convenient and healthy port than Poti, Sir Edward thus drew the following conclusions as to the advantages to be derived from the new route thus constituted:—"From Odessa," he continued, "troops can be conveyed across the Black Sea to Batoum in two days, from thence by rail to Baku in twenty-four hours, another twenty-four hours would see them landed at Krasnovodsk, transferred in lighters to the shallow water to Michaelovsk, and the entrainment of them begun, when the journey to Kizil Arvat, the present but by no means the final terminus of the Transcaspian line, occupies twelve hours.

"The communication with Odessa, of course, admits of the reinforcement of the Caucasian army to any extent. But the Caucasus itself forms an effectively independent territory for beginning a campaign. It is no wild, barbarous region, but a country rich, well-watered, and now thoroughly Russian, and its capital, Tiflis, in the advantages of its site and climate, its public and private buildings, and its establishment as the head-quarters of an army, may stand comparison with nearly any city in the Czar's dominions. The war strength of the army of the Caucasus is 160,000 men.

"The efficacy of the other channel of communication between Russia and the Caspian has also been largely increased of late years. Besides four lines of railway to points on the Volga, complete communication between the Neva and that river is afforded by the canal system of the country. And to obviate the interruption occurring in the winter months, a line of railway is projected from a point where many lines from Russia converge, in Cis-Caucasia, to Petrovsk on the Caspian, and thence along its shore to Baku. You will therefore probably agree that there is not at present much difficulty, and that such as there is will shortly disappear, either in bringing reserves and stores, to any extent, on the lines from Northern Russia, and also from Southern Russia, to the Caspian, or in conveying the army of the Caucasus with its stores from that sea to the Transcaspian railway, and along that line to Kizil Arvat. That terminus is 135 miles from Askabad, to which place the railway will doubtless be carried. Askabad is 186 miles from Sarakhs and Sarakhs is 202 from Herát, only a few miles more than the distance from York to London."

I make no apology for this quotation, for the words of which it is composed present in the fairest and clearest light to the reader the immense advantages which Skobeleff's victory at Geok Tepé, and the consequent annexation of the Transcaspian territory, has procured for Russia. That territory is united now by the speediest of all modern modes of communication with St. Petersburg, with Moscow, and with all the great arsenals of Russia. That conquest brought not an isolated and outlying portion of Russia—but the whole Russian empire bound into one solid mass by the iron road, as near to Herát, within a few miles as the most advanced outposts of British India! As we go on we shall see that the evil did not stop there!

Nor was the power to concentrate an irresistible force upon the furthest point of its Transcaspian territory the only advantage gained for his country by Skobeleff at Geok Tepé. Leaving absolutely out of consideration the prestige, the moral influence—though that is a factor which must enter largely into the calculation of a statesman when he has to deal with Eastern peoples—there remain two distinct material advantages, both of which will affect very powerfully any struggle which may occur in Afghánistán or

* Kizil Arvat is 523 miles from Herát; the British outposts are 514.

on the existing British frontier, between Russia and Great Britain. These are (1), the enormous influence gained by the former over Persia; (2) the employment as the vanguard of her armies of the conquered Turkomans.

With respect to the first I shall again quote from the same competent authority, to whose warnings in May of last year the country turned a deaf ear. "Next to her resources for a campaign," said Sir Edward Hamley on that occasion, "Russia's relations with Persia are of prime importance." Describing then the various phases of the attitude of Persia towards Russia between 1876 and 1880, Sir Edward thus continued: "But, in the following year, after Skobeleff had established himself at Bámi, a remarkable change occurred in the attitude of Persia. Ostensible orders to the contrary notwithstanding, he was allowed to procure vast supplies of provisions from Khorásán; and when, after the capture of Geok Tepé, he marched beyond Askabad in pursuit, he was allowed to violate Persian territory without remonstrance, and the Turkomans who escaped into what they supposed to be the neutral territory of Persia were handed over as prisoners to the Russians. In fact how can Persia, without the strongest support, resist such a neighbour? The Russian border is co-terminous with hers from Mount Ararat to beyond Askabad. The fleet on the Caspian and the new railway give Russia the means of invading at a hundred points the bordering territory, furnishing a hundred good reasons why Persia could no more oppose the will of Russia than the mere human being of her own tales could oppose the tremendous spirit who rose in clouds from the sea, or descended on over-shadowing wings from the sky." Information which has been received since the lecture from which this passage is quoted was delivered, and since the Russian advances to Merv and Sarakhs, therein foreshadowed, have become accomplished facts, goes to prove that at the present moment Persia is an inert mass to be moulded at will by her powerful neighbour.

The second advantage I have referred to—the incorporation of the Turkoman cavalry in the Russian army has been also already accomplished. The rule of terror, always an initial factor with Russia when dealing with Oriental races, did its work, as I have already said, at Geok Tepé. That crushing defeat and the unsparing manner with which it was followed, broke the free spirit of the desert-born warriors. Recognizing in their subduers their masters, they accepted their fate, and they are now ready to forage, to fight, and to plunder for the successors to the empire of Nadir Sháh!

I return from this digression—a digression necessary to display the great results obtained by Russia from Skobeleff's triumph at Geok Tepé—to describe the further progress made in the Transcaspian line of conquest. I left the Russian army pursuing the Turkomans as far as Askabad, only 388 miles from Herát. I propose now to describe their further progress since that date.

The victory of Geok Tepé had subdued for ever, a very important tribe of the Turkomans, the Akhal Tekkes. But there were other tribes scarcely less formidable. These were the Sarik Turkomans, numbering 65,000 souls, lying along the Murgháb river between Merv and Herát; the Tejend Turkomans, occupying the country watered by the river of that name to within thirty miles of Sarakhs; and the Merv Tekkes or the tribe which pastured its herds round about Merv. All these tribes were to be absorbed.

The turn of the Tejend Turkomans came first. Terrified by the defeat of their brethren at Geok Tepé and its consequences, they offered, almost on the morrow of the victory, their submission to the conquerors. That submission brought into the possession of Russia the Tejend oasis, a territory, to use the words of Lieutenant, now, I believe, Colonel, Alikhanoff, who surveyed it, "almost larger than that of Merv," and brought her within striking distance—30 miles—of Sarakhs, and within 232 of Herát. The Tejend river which waters that oasis is, in very deed, the Heri-rúd which waters Herát, for, flowing northwards as it approaches the Persian frontier near Kuhsan, it takes, just beyond Pul-i-Khátun, the name of the swamp in which it finally disappears. It forms then, if not a water road to Herát, yet a road which supplies troops marching along its banks with one of the two primary necessities for an army.

For a time after that submission Russia remained apparently quiescent. She was only biding her time. Whilst the attention of the politicians of England was fixed upon the events passing in Egypt and in the Soudan, they read one morning in January, 1884, that Merv had been occupied. Some years before, even statesmen who believed in the promises of Russia, had declared that her troops could never be allowed to occupy Merv. Yet in 1884, that occupation was allowed to pass with but a feeble protest!

The full significance of that important acquisition is not even yet properly appreciated by the governing classes and the people of these islands. In vain did two Englishmen and one foreigner attempt to rouse them to a sense of the danger it involved. One of these, Mr. Charles Marvin, whose services in respect of the Russo-Afghan question have been invaluable, and who, speaking and writing with absolute knowledge personally acquired, can understand better than any living man the feelings of the Cassandra of the Homeric legend, published at once a pamphlet* in

* "The Russian Annexation of Merv." W. H. Allen & Co.

which he dwelt emphatically upon the opportunities which such a movement gave to Russia. "The conquest of Merv," wrote Mr. Marvin, in February, 1884, "is something more than the annexation of a mid-desert oasis. It means the complete junction of the military forces of the Caucasus and Turkestán. It means, with the annexation of Akhal, the absorption of 100,000 of the best Irregular cavalry in the world, at a week's march from the city of Herát. It means the meeting, for the first time, of the Cossack and the Afghán. It means the complete enclosure of Khiva within the Russian empire, and the reduction of Bokhára from the independent position of a border state to the dependence of an incorporated province. It means the enclosure of more than 200,000 square miles of territory, and the addition to the Russian empire of a region as large as France. It means the completion of the conquest of the Central Asian deserts, and the commencement of the annexation of the great fertile mountain region of Persia and Afghánistán. It means the deliberate occupation of a strategical point, fraught with political entanglements of such a wide-spread nature, that, whether Russia desire it or not, she will be inevitably led, unless forestalled or checked by England, to Meshed, to Herát, to Balkh, and to Kábul. And she will not remain there. She will continue her swift advance until she triumphantly lays down her Cossack border alongside the Sepoy line of India."

It may be objected by some that these are the opinions of Mr. Marvin, and that they do not care to listen to Mr. Marvin, because, when the Conservatives were in office he was charged with divulging information which compromised the Government. I may remark, in passing, that that charge in no way affects the credibility of a man who has heard with his own ears the opinions expressed on the subject by Russian generals and Russian diplomatists, and who, for the love of England, has spent his own money to warn England's people. But let us turn from Mr. Marvin, from this past-master of the history of Transcaspian aggression, and read what the greatest strategist of England has to say upon the subject.

"Commercially viewed," said Sir Edward Hamley in the lecture from which I have already quoted, delivered in May of last year, "Russia has gained in Merv for the present merely a fresh burthen. The Turkomans, debarred from brigandage, and unfit for any sustained commercial or agricultural enterprises, will be but an impoverished community. They possess no towns nor institutions, nor territories which exhibit any mark either of prosperity or of the faculty of becoming prosperous. The one advantage of the possession is that the caravan route passing Bokhára to Meshed and the interior, and that from India by Herát to Central Asia, lie through Merv. But that it was once a centre of great prosperity is proved by the fact that the remains of four great cities exist there, the inhabitants of the last of which were driven out by the present semi-barbarians about a century ago. Under Russian rule that prosperity will revive—the land will once more teem with the crops to which nothing is wanting but good husbandry. And, when once again become populous and fertile, it will afford a secondary base against the Afghán frontier. In the meanwhile it closes the gap aforesaid, and as soon as Russia lays down her frontier line, the whole of that vast empire from the Baltic to the Danube, thence along the Black Sea, across the Caucasus to the Caspian, along the Persian frontier to Merv and Turkistán, and so on to Siberia, will lie in a ring fence. This is the Power which is now separated from a frontier which, presumably, we cannot allow her to overstep, by a borderland which is a barrier in no sense, and which I will endeavour briefly to describe."

On the same subject, Sir Charles Macgregor wrote in 1875:—"There is no doubt in my mind that the real danger lies in our permitting the Russians to concentrate unopposed at Merv, which is quite within *coup de main* distance of Herát; and it is in this fact, and in this alone, that the value of Merv to the Russians lies. Once place Herát beyond the possibility of a *coup de main*, and I cannot imagine the astute statesmen of Russia persisting in the occupation of an isolated spot in the desert, the maintenance of which must cost a great deal." The forecast has been already proved true!

It will be observed that Sir Edward Hamley speaks of the new frontier as one "which, presumably, we cannot allow her (Russia) to overstep." But six months had not elapsed since the delivery of the lecture when Russia did take another step forward—a step, in my opinion, the most important of all subsequent to the victory of Geok Tepé. In the autumn of last year Russia advanced her outposts along the Persian frontier from Askabad to Sarakhs!

Russia would not have been Russia had she not accompanied this most important move onward by the usual attempt to deceive the gullible British public, and their worse than gullible representatives in the House of Commons. I shall show more clearly further on why the plea was that there was an old Sarakhs and a new Sarakhs, was of all pleas the most disingenuous. Russia gained the position on the bank of the Tejend most convenient to her for an operation against Herát, and the value of that position was, as I shall show, in no way affected by the fact that she did not occupy the fort as well! Yet the excuse, lame as it was, went down: it was accepted; and Russia was allowed to remain at old Sarakhs without even a remonstrance!

The enormous importance of this step has never been sufficiently appreciated. With all humility and with all earnestness I would beg my countrymen to turn for a moment from the selfish strife of parties, and devote a few minutes' consideration to a subject which affects, and vitally affects, the future position of the British Empire. The position occupied by old Sarakhs ought never to have been allowed to fall into the hands of Russia. That she was allowed to take it is a proof of the state of vassalage to which Persia has been reduced, for new and old Sarakhs constituted a frontier post of that country. Let us, for a moment, examine their position.

Fortunately, we are able, on this subject, to write "from the book." In 1875, one of the ablest and most accomplished officers who wear the British uniform, the present Quartermaster-General of Her Majesty's army in India, Major-General Sir Charles MacGregor, visited Sarakhs. There is no uncertainty in the opinion he gave regarding its value. "A glance at the map will show," he wrote, "that in the complication which must arise ere the Russo-Indian question can be deemed settled, its future—'the future of Sarakhs'—is likely to be a stirring one. Placed at the junction of roads from Herát and Meshed, by the Heri-rúd and Ab-i-Meshed valleys respectively, and at the best entrance to the province of Khorásán from the north, it cannot fail to exercise a very serious influence on the momentous issue of the above question. This must happen, whether it fall into the hands of the friends of England or into those of her foes. Whether Russia use Sarakhs as a base for offensive measures against Herát, or England use her as a defensive outpost to defeat any such operations, that position will be heard of again. And if my feeble voice can effect a warning, ere it is too late let it here be raised in these words:—*If England does not use Sarakhs for defence Russia will use it for offence.*"*

I am no alarmist. The words I have quoted are the words of a very able man who has spent his life on the Indian frontier, who can speak the language of the Afgháns and the Khorásánis, a man who has ever kept his eyes and his ears well open. The journal of his travels teems with evidence that even in those days Persia was being Russianized. There is not a soldier living who knows MacGregor who would not accept as an absolute truth his warning words about Sarakhs. And yet, the English Government allowed Russia to take quietly and without remonstrance the plains commanding that most important place—a place which is an eye to see and an arm to strike. When a faint voice was raised in Parliament upon the question it was silenced by the disingenuous plea, already referred to, that there were two such places known as Sarakhs, and that the Sarakhs occupied was not the fortress but the old town!

Is there an old town of Sarakhs? There was indeed in earlier days an old Sarakhs, but there is but one fortified town now. Let the reader follow the description of Sir Charles MacGregor:—"The scene that met my eye" he writes, describing his survey of the country from the north tower of the only existing Sarakhs, "is easily described. To the north stretched one vast plain, which, except for a few mounds and a ruined mosque marking the site of one of the former towns of Sarakhs, was unbroken by tree, bush, mound, or undulations as far as the eye could reach. The Tejend, it is true, winds round to the

* The italics are Sir Charles MacGregor's. *Vide* "Narrative of a Journey through the Province of Khorassan and the N.W. Frontier of Afghanistan in 1875." London: W. H. Allen & Co., 1879.

north-west, but its bed is low, below the level of the plain, and so nothing can be seen of it. It was a strange feeling to look out on this wild interminable expanse, and think that for an arc of 80°, there was not for 300 miles perhaps one single drop of water, or one human being. To the north-east lay the road to Merv stretched out beyond the dark tamarisk foliage in the bed of the Tejend. To the east all was clear: to the south-east were undulating rounded ridges (covered with little black dots which they told me were "pista" bushes)* extending towards the Murgháb. To the south was the Múzduran ridge we had come through, and a little way north of west was a confused mass of rugged ridges, among which I was informed lay the famed stronghold of the great Nadir."

This plain on the Tejend, then, is really the position of Sarakhs? That position Russia has taken and Russia holds. It is idle to argue that the position is valueless because she does not hold also the fort of Sarakhs. The fort of Sarakhs "has a garrison" (I quote again from MacGregor) "of one battalion of infantry, numbering some seven hundred men, eleven guns, good, bad, and indifferent, and a few horsemen; but the dimensions of the fort are such that it would take ten times this number to man the walls, even in the most inefficient manner." In a word, the Russians can walk into it whenever they may choose to do so!

MacGregor gives us, likewise, a plan and description of the fortress. He then adds:—"Were the Turkoman question for ever at rest"—Russia has settled it since he penned those words—"I see no reason why Sarakhs should not become a place of considerable importance as a large

* The Pistachio nut.

population could easily be supported by agriculture alone, and its convenient position with reference to Meshed and Herát on the south, and Khiva and Bokhára on the north, marks it out a future probable entrepôt of commerce." Further on, he adds: "Commercially, it is admirably situated for drawing to it all the trade between Turkistán on the north and Khorasán on the south; and it has every advantage of soil and water and climate that would be necessary for these purposes."

On the same subject—the position of Sarakhs—let us study the description of the position as given by the correspondent of the *Illustrated London News*, in the issue of that paper of the 14th March:—

"Sarakhs, which the Russians were permitted to occupy soon after their conquest of Merv, and from which the understood line of Afghan boundary was to have been drawn eastward to the Oxus by the Joint Commission, consists of old and new Sarakhs, three miles and a half apart, situated on opposite sides of the Heri-rud, the bed of which, at that particular place, was dry at the season when the British Commission arrived there. This place belonged to Persia, but old Sarakhs, on the eastern side, was handed over to the Russians by the Persian Governor. When our Special Artist visited old Sarakhs, the Russian Governor-General of the Transcaspian Provinces, General Komaroff, was there, but only a few Russian troops, who were Akhal Turkomans recently enlisted in the Russian army. The sketch now given shows the remains of the old city, which is entirely deserted; to the east and north there are a number of reed huts with a few people living in them. Old Sarakhs, as the sketch will show, is merely a square mound, rising high above the present level of the desert, and this mound is no doubt an accumulation of rubbish formed by the destruction of houses and the re-building of them during a long course of time. The ruined walls of one building are all that stands of the old town; the rest of the space is a mass of bricks and weeds. The walls are of burned brick, but are in a very crumbling state. The town itself evidently has not had an inhabitant for many years. On the north and east are the remains of crumbling mud walls, which may have been inhabited since the old city was left to decay. The old tomb seen to the right of this view is called Baba Ogle; but there is a tradition that it is the tomb of Abel, the tomb of Cain being at new Sarakhs.

"New Sarakhs, which is still occupied by the Persians, is on the western bank of the Heri-rud, 300 yards from the river bed. It is of late date, and is possessed of the usual mud walls, with towers. The wall encloses a space of 700 yards diameter. The governor, Ali Mardan Khan, who has to deal with the whole of the frontier of this part of Persia, lives in the town, and has four or five hundred troops. Although the walls cover a good amount of ground, there are very few people in the place. In the sketch, the mound of old Sarakhs is just visible in the distance; in the foreground is one of the usual towers of refuge. Mr. Simpson made a separate sketch of the Meshed Gate of new Sarakhs, which shows the character of the crenelated walls and the towers. There are only two gates to the town—this gate, and another towards the north, called the Bokhára gate. Inside of the Meshed gate is the Arg, or citadel, where the governor lives, and the garrison have their quarters. A wall separates this from the other part of the town. There is a ditch perhaps 10 feet or 12 feet deep, and nearly 20 feet wide, round the walls, with a covered way, or *chemin de ronde*, between the wall and the ditch. There are six small brass guns placed at various points, but the mud walls could offer no defence to a regular attack.

"A curious feature of the river above Sarakhs is the dam, or 'bund,' as it would be termed in India, at Kizil Koi, by which the water is diverted into streams for artificial irrigation. Kizil-Koi is eight miles higher up the river, between Sarakhs and Pul-i-Khátun. This dam, which is a very primitive affair, being made of wattles and earth, fills a water-course, which supplies old Sarakhs; and new Sarakhs receives its supply of water on the other side of the Heri-Rud from a point not far distant. All cultivation in this region is done by means of irrigation derived from rivers and Streams; and the protection of "water supply" is an important part of the frontier question. On the ordinary maps it will be seen that the Heriserai is on the Persian side of the bridge, standing on the right bank of the Kershef-Rud. The date of its erection is given as in Timour's time. The view taken by me is looking south, and the high hills forming the background are all on the Persian side. The Kershef-Rud is a small stream which enters the Heri-Rud on its left bank only a few yards below the bridge."

Let the reader realize the commercial and military advantages of this position; further, that the fortress resting on that position belongs to a prince who is virtually a vassal of Russia; further still, that the position, capable of a large development, lies by the valley of the Heri-rúd, 202 miles, by the alternative route along the Murgháb valley, a somewhat shorter distance, from Herát: that it is about 60 miles from Merv, and *that the routes from the two places to Herát, by the Murgháb valley, converge at Panjdeh*; let him realise all this, and then ask with surprise under what blind infatuation has the British Government permitted the occupation of these two threatening positions, Merv and Sarakhs, by a colossal power which is advancing towards India, without making a corresponding forward movement from the Indus?

The consideration of this infatuation will form the subject of the next chapter.

CHAPTER V.

THE INFATUATION OF GREAT BRITAIN.

THE Ministers of the Crown of Great Britain and Ireland are, or are supposed to be, the executors of the will of the people of these islands. However culpably ignorant and culpably inefficient a ministry may be, it is unfair then absolutely to condemn them if the people whom they represent absolve them. If the people of these islands are misgoverned, if they sanction a policy which tends to the loss of India, they have mainly themselves to blame. In describing "the infatuation of Great Britain" I shall describe a course of conduct which, though initiated by the minister, has been sanctioned by the people. It is to the people that I appeal. I tell them that that policy which they have sanctioned is risking the loss of their greatest dependency. I implore them not to be blinded by oratorical platitudes, but to look facts sternly in the face. I make this appeal not as a party-man, for it will be seen I blame both parties, but as an Englishman who loves his country and who feels that the empire which has been created by the valour, by the energy, by the skill, and by the devotion of our forefathers can only be maintained by the display of the same qualities by their descendants!

At the close of the third chapter I brought the action of the British Government up to the year 1869, the year in which, Samarkhand having been annexed and Bokhára controlled by Russia, Lord Clarendon made his famous proposition for constituting Afghánistán as a neutral zone, and received in reply Prince Gortschakoff's assurance, that his master, the Czar, "looks upon Afghánistán as completely without the sphere in which Russia may be called upon to exercise her influence."* I added, that on the Government of India objecting to an arrangement which would remove Afghánistán completely from the sphere of British influence, the negotiations with Russia were prolonged for two years, the Russian Government continuing to protest, by the mouth of its Chancellor, that "Russia had no intention of going further south," and that "extension of territory was extension of weakness." I shewed further that with these honied terms upon her lips Russia was, during those two years, preparing for the spring upon Khiva which she made in 1873. I now propose to resume the history of the recent negotiations of the Governments of Great Britain and India from the period, January 1869, when Sher Ali, having overcome all his rivals, became unquestioned ruler of Afghánistán.

In the autumn immediately preceding his decisive victory in January 1869 over his relative, Abdul Rahman, the victorious Amir, Sher Ali, believing his authority to be permanently established, requested the Lieutenant-Governor of the Punjáb, Sir Donald Macleod, to inform the Viceroy—the late Lord Lawrence—that, in order to concert a good understanding between the two Governments it would be a satisfaction to himself if the Viceroy would meet him at Pesháwur or some other place on the frontier. The Viceroy was willing to grant the interview, and would have arranged it, but, before preliminaries could be settled, there occurred that invasion by Abdul Rahman, the repelling of which demanded all the energies of Sher Ali.

Two months after the decisive battle which confirmed Sher Ali on his throne Lord Lawrence left India. His successor, the Earl of Mayo, possessed the rare and difficult gift of a thorough knowledge of his fellow-men. He was quick, beyond all men whom I have met, in reading character. This gift, joined to great decision and energy, would have made him under any circumstances a strong man. But, added to it, and gilding, as it were, all his actions, there was a singular charm of manner, which impressed everyone with whom he came in contact, and which was sure to exercise, and which did exercise, a remarkable influence over an Oriental people.

One of the first acts of the new Viceroy was to examine the relations existing between India, and the ruler of the mountainous region on its north-western border. Realising at once the importance of the interview which Sher Ali had solicited from his predecessor, Lord Mayo at once forwarded to him an invitation to meet him at Ambála. The invitation was accepted.

Sher Ali came to Ambála in the spring of 1869. Had the hands of Lord Mayo been free, it is quite possible that an arrangement might have been arrived at which would have prevented the second Afghan war and have rendered impossible Russian aggression. But Lord Mayo's hands were tied very tightly indeed. Shortly after his acceptance of the office of Viceroy, the Minister who had recommended him for that office had been displaced; and there had come into power a Ministry upon whom a phrase invented by Lord Lawrence, the phrase "masterly inactivity," exercised a fascination which its very victims would find it now difficult to explain. The real meaning of this phrase, as interpreted by the action of those who adopted it, was that Russia might do as she pleased in Central Asia, provided she did not touch Afghánistán; whilst British India should remain inactive, not encumbering herself with an offensive alliance with a power beyond its actual frontier, least of all with Afghánistán, and taking care to give no pledge to support the dynasty of the actual ruler of that country.

If we bear in mind this fettered position of Lord Mayo, we shall easily recognize the greatness of the disappointment likely to accrue to the Amir Sher Ali. For Sher Ali had come to Ambála full of hope of obtaining the support which a dependent ruler has a right to expect from his suzerain. Sher Ali had come to Ambála hopeful of securing an offensive and defensive alliance with the Government of India. He desired a full assurance of protection against Russian aggression, the prospects of which, ever since the fall of Samarkhand, had filled him with apprehension. He wished to be assured, in a distinct and absolute manner, that the British would recognize as his successor, in his own lifetime, the son whom he was prepared to nominate. These were the cardinal aims which had prompted him to solicit an interview from Lord Lawrence, and which influenced him to accept the invitation of Lord Mayo. He had come to Ambála in the full hope that his wishes with respect to all of them would be gratified. Even we, who are behind the scenes, and who know how completely the hands of Lord Mayo were tied, cannot realize the full measure of the disappointment in store for him.

The charm of Lord Mayo's manner won indeed the heart of the man, but the spirit of his replies wounded to the quick the soul of the Amir. With respect to Sher Ali's demand for a specific promise of full protection against Russian aggression, Lord Mayo could reply only with the vague promise that "he would be strengthened from time to time as circumstances might seem to require;" that his applications for assistance would always be received "with consideration and respect." Nor, on the domestic question, was the answer he received one whit more satisfactory to the Amír. He was not even solaced with a promise that he would be supported against any attempt which his rivals might make to unseat him. The utmost he could obtain was an assurance that any attempt on their part would be regarded by the British Government with "severe displeasure;" whilst as to the recognition of his favourite son as his successor, although, with respect to that, he made—to use Lord Mayo's expression—"the most urgent and prominent demands;" stated his earnest wish that the Government of India "should acknowledge not only himself, but his lineal descendants or successors in blood;" and added that, if this were accorded "there was nothing he would not do to evince his gratitude," he was met, as far as Lord Mayo was concerned, by a reluctant "*non possumus!*"

Sher Ali returned to Kábul a sincere admirer and personal friend of Lord Mayo, but utterly disappointed with the political results of his journey. To all intents and purposes he was in a position, with respect to British support, but little better than that which he had occupied when he accepted the invitation. He vented his feelings in the bitter remark: "The English care only for themselves!"

Yet—and it is a remarkable result of the glamour exercised by those fatal words "masterly inactivity"—even the vague assurances of Lord Mayo had excited the alarm of the Ministry in England. The phrase used by the Viceroy that any application for assistance on the part of the Amir, would be received "with consideration and respect" was objected to by the Minister for India, on the ground that those words "may some day be construed by the Amir or by his successors as meaning more than, with those explanations"—*i.e.*, the verbal explanations given by Lord Mayo to the Amir—"they were intended to convey." The same Minister even wrote a despatch to the Viceroy, in which, amongst other matters, he objected to the term "rightful rule" as applied to the rule of Sher Ali over Afghánistán!

Time went on. The Russian Government, after amusing for more than two years the British Ministry with vague and specious promises, struck at and captured Khiva, in 1873. The news of this capture reached Kábul in June of the same year. It filled the mind of the Amir with terror. The catastrophe which he had seen looming in the future at Ambála had come upon him. Khiva had followed Samarkhand. The turn of Afghánistán would follow Full of these apprehensions he stretched out his hands to the Viceroy, telling him that the vague assurances of Ambála were insufficient for the present emergency, and desiring to know how far he might rely upon British help if he should be invaded.

It was, surely, a natural request, this solicitation from the commander of the outer bulwark of Hindustan to the ruler of the country which that bulwark covered. It was a request which should have received a sympathizing and reassuring reply.

The Viceroy of India was no longer Lord Mayo. That nobleman had been assassinated in the Andamans by a convict sentenced to penal servitude for murder, and had been succeeded by Lord Northbrook, a man whose cold unsympathizing manners and hard unimaginative nature were not calculated to conciliate.

Lord Northbrook did not feel empowered to reply to the message of the Amir, but referred it by telegram to the Ministry at home, the same Ministry which had adopted with respect to India the fatal principle summed up in the Lawrentian motto. The reply he received is worth recording as a specimen of the "masterly imbecility" which pervaded British councils in July 1873.

"Cabinet thinks," so ran the telegram, "you should inform Amir that we do not at all share his alarm, and consider there is no cause for it; but you may assure him we shall maintain our settled policy in favour of Afghánistán if he abides your advice in external affairs."

The Khanáte of Khiva annexed, and no cause for alarm! Surely that was cold comfort for a ruler who, on the spot, possessed the best means for judging! "We do not share his alarm." We—who have been duped by this very act of Russia; who were told that the expedition was a very little one, that far from its being the intention of the Czar to take Khiva, positive orders had been sent to prevent it; we, who, after the event, do not care to examine "too minutely how far these arrangements were in strict accordance with the assurances given in January;" we, who have been duped at every turn and who have been wrong in every forecast—we "do not at all share his alarm, and consider there is no cause for it!" Cold comfort that, I repeat, coming from such a quarter, for an anxious and alarmed ruler!

Cold comfort indeed Sher Ali found it. Such a message was calculated to confirm rather than to remove his fears, But he did not even then despair. He would place before the Governor-General, and, through him, before the British Government, facts which should speak, and he would make a final appeal to their justice and to their interests. In this intent, Sher Ali transmitted fresh instructions to an agent whom he had previously despatched to Simla, the summer residence of the Viceroy, a nobleman who enjoyed all his confidence, Saiad Nur Muhammad Sháh, urging him to press for certain definite concessions on the two matters which he himself had so strongly urged at Ambála, viz., the absolute assurance of suppor against Russia when he should demand it, and the recognition of his favourite son as his successor.

Nur Muhammad Sháh carried out these instructions to the letter. He had had one interview with Lord Northbrook on the 12th July: a second was accorded to him on the 30th. So far as related to the calming of the apprehensions or satisfying the demands of the Amir these interviews were absolutely unproductive. Their result may be summed up in a letter addressed by order of the Viceroy to the Amir. In that letter the Amir was informed that whilst the Viceroy did not entertain any apprehension of danger to his Highness's dominions from without, yet that "the the British Government will endeavour from time to time, by such means as circumstances may require, to strengthen the Government of your Highness, to enable you to exercise with equity and justice your rightful rule, and to transmit to your descendants all the dignities and honours of which you are the lawful possessor." In the same letter *the Amir was reminded of the assurances given by Russia as to his country being quite beyond the sphere within which she was called upon to exercise her influence.* Basing his decision on that assurance, Lord Northbrook "postponed to a more convenient opportunity" the discussion of the measures to be taken in the event of an attack upon Afghánistán!

In the mind of Sher Ali this letter was a deathblow to all his expectations. Let us for a moment realize his position. He ruled the middle region between two colossal powers, England and Russia. Every reason, geographical position, personal feeling, his knowledge of the practical justice of her rule in India, prompted him to link his lot with the former. But Russia was advancing with giant strides. She was within striking distance of his eastern border at Samarkhand; the capture of Khiva had ensured to her a position which must sooner or later bring her on to his western frontier; her agents were busy throughout Central Asia dwelling upon her power and boasting of her intentions; he wished to be in a position to be able to defy alike her promises and her threats. In reply to his demand to be placed in such a position, he received only general assurances that he had no ground for his alarm.

That the Amir was right in construing as evasive the reply of Lord Northbrook is proved by the letter from that nobleman to the Secretary of State for India explaining its meaning. In that letter the Viceroy stated that the envoy of the Amir had been informed that "if, in the event *of any aggression from without, British influence were invoked, and failed by negotiation to effect a satisfactory settlement, IT WAS PROBABLE that the British Government would afford the Amir material assistance in repelling an invader;* but that such assistance would be conditional on the Amir following the advice of the British Government, and having himself abstained from aggression."

Observe: the above is the Viceroy's own interpretation of his own reply to the Amir! Was it a reply calculated to reassure? Was it a reply worthy of the occasion, worthy of a statesman? Here was the commander of the outlying bulwark telling the Governor of the rich city which it covered that he dreaded the sudden attack of a subtle enemy, and begging for a definite assurance that he would be protected. In reply the Governor refuses to *promise* him protection: tells him only that if he were attacked negotiation would first be tried; that then, if negotiation were to fail, there was—not a certainty let it be noted—but *a probability* that he would be protected: and that only if he were to comply with certain conditions!

Mark these conditions. The first: that he should follow the advice of the British Government: truly a hard condition, for the British Government might have advised him to yield a Pul-i-Khátun or a Panjdeh in order to retain the remainder of his dominions. The second condition was harder still. "That he should himself have abstained from aggression." Nothing easier in words, nothing more difficult, in the presence of Russia, in practice. The straying of a few herdsmen across the border might be termed aggression. The history of Russia, and her connection with the states she has swallowed up, is a constant repetition of the story of the wolf and the lamb!

Looking back at that unhappy episode, I cannot believe that the most prominent British actors in it would care to defend it. The reply of the Viceroy was ungenerous, unstatesmanlike, and unworthy. It produced the only possible result which a clear-headed man could have anticipated from it. It alienated the Amir from England, and disposed him to receive with favour the advances of Russia. His sense of the unworthy tone of Lord Northbrook's letter, with its assurances of probable assistance in case he should be attacked, found vent in the sarcastic reply which he transmitted: "The friendly declaration of your Excellency," he wrote in November of the same year, "to the effect that you will maintain towards me the same policy which was followed by Lord Lawrence and by Lord Mayo, has been the cause of much gratification to me. My friend! Under these circumstances of the case it was not necessary to hold all those conversations with Saiad Nur Muhammad Sháh! The understanding arrived at at Ambála is quite sufficient"! From that moment his confidential correspondence with the Viceroy ceased. "I am determined," he said, "to receive no more favours from the British Government!"

Russia meanwhile was continuing her mole-like work in Central Asia. The fruit of this work was next seen in

February 1876, when she absorbed the remaining moiety of Khokand, permitting only the principality of Karatighin to retain a condition of semi-independence.

In the spring of that year Lord Lytton succeeded Lord Northbrook as Viceroy of India. The new Viceroy came out empowered by his Government to repair, if it were possible, the mischief which had been accomplished, by offering to the Amir the active support and protection, including the formal recognition of his dynasty, which he had previously vainly demanded at the hands of the British Government. But before Lord Lytton had been able to open communications with the Amir, certain events had happened which had confirmed that potentate in the hostile attitude which he had assumed after the mission of Saiad Nur Muhammad Sháh in 1873.

There had been a dispute of long standing between Afghánistán and Persia regarding certain lands in Sëistán, the south-western province of the former state. In the end both powers had agreed to refer the matter to the arbitration of England. Shortly before Lord Lytton landed in India, the arbitrators had given a decision very much in favour of Persia. This result of a difference in which he believed that all the right was on his side so embittered the Amir that, coming as it did after the Simla conferences, he attributed it to a settled design on the part of England to humiliate, to weaken, and to insult him.

The action of the Government of India in another matter on which he was extremely sensitive still further embittered the Amir against the British.

The son who had accompanied Sher Ali to Ambála in 1870, and on whose behalf he had pleaded to Lord Mayo, was his youngest boy, Abdúla Ján, born to him by his favourite wife. Popular sympathy had however been excited in Afghánistán and in India in favour of an elder son,

Yakúb Khán, at the time governor of Herát, and who was believed to be endowed with more than ordinary ability. This general impression as to the capacity of Yakúb Khán tended, in the belief of the Amir, to the disparagement of his favourite in public estimation. His first act, therefore, on his return from the Ambála conference, had been to entice Yahúb Khán to Kábul, and to throw him into a dungeon. This act was so far resented by the Government of India that it never failed to press upon the Amir it's opinion of the injustice and impolicy of his action, and to urge the release of the prisoner. This constant remonstrance, coming after all the Amir's requests had been denied, had engendered feelings which the decision regarding Sëistán increased to positive hatred.

The Amir was under the influence of this passion when Lord Lytton arrived in India. One of the first political acts of the new Viceroy was to despatch a native Aide-de-camp to Kábul with a message of reconciliation. But the evil had been done. Sher Ali had already taken his part. There were at the time Russian agents in Kábul, agents who readily promised what the English had refused, and who had therefore entire possession of his mind. Sher Ali declined then, ostentatiously, to receive the messenger of the Viceroy, and though the conciliatory language of Lord Lytton rendered it impossible for him to refuse the proposal that a conference between two duly-empowered envoys from the two courts should take place at Pesháwar, he took care to furnish his envoy with instructions which should render the negotiations fruitless.

The interview between the two negotiators took place at Pesháwar in the early part of 1877. England was represented on that occasion by Sir Lewis Pelly, a very distinguished officer, who, had some years before, made the journey, alone, wearing all the time the British uniform, from Teheran to the British frontier, crossing a dangerous corner of Afghanistan, and who was thoroughly acquainted with the habits, language, and modes of thought of the people. To that able officer it soon became apparent that, since 1873, the *rôles* of the negociators had been inverted. In that year it had been the British Viceroy who had declined all the propositions of the Amir: in 1877, it was the representative of Kábul who refused his assent to the terms of accommodation and reconciliation set forth by the representative of the British Government. To such an extent did this proceed, so unaccommodating—even hostile—did the language of the Kábul envoy at last become, that the Viceroy wisely took advantage of the death of that nobleman to declare the conference at an end.

From that moment the Government of India, acting upon instructions from England, resolved "to maintain an attitude of vigilant reserve until such time as the Amir might better realize his own position and interests." This policy was persevered in for twenty months. During that period the aggressive action of Russia continued to develop itself. There cannot be a doubt but that, had the negotiations between England and Russia in 1878 terminated in a rupture between the two powers, Russia was prepared to follow in the footsteps of Nádir Sháh—to threaten from the base of a friendly Afghánistán the empire of Hindustan. Under these circumstances, it was not possible that the British Government should remain quiescent, when—a breach between Russia and England seeming to be a question not of days but of hours—the Amir received with remarkable ostentation an embassy despatched to him by the Czar!

Yet though it was impossible that the British Government should allow to pass without notice an act which constituted a breach of the engagement existing between itself and the Amir—the engagement made between Dost Muhammed and Mr. John Lawrence in 1854, accepted by Sher Ali on his accession, confirmed by him at Ambála in 1870, and never subsequently abrogated—the engagement that he would be "the friend of the friends and the enemy of the enemies" of the British Government—the notice which the Viceroy did take of it was remarkable for its moderation. Lord Lytton simply required that the Amir, having welcomed an embassy from the Czar, should receive in his capital an embassy from the Viceroy of British India. He informed the Amir at the same time that his refusal would be construed as an unfriendly, even as a hostile, act.

The conduct of Sher Ali on receiving the friendly letter containing this proposal from the Viceroy was more than discourteous. Not only did he vouchsafe to it no reply, but he directed the officer commanding the advanced posts in the direction of the British frontier to refuse admission to the British envoy and his retinue, and, if necessary, to repel him by force!

The Viceroy, meanwhile, had directed the distinguished officer whom he had nominated to be envoy—General Sir Neville Chamberlain—to proceed on his mission. But when Chamberlain attempted to enter the Khaibar pass he found its heights occupied by the army of the Amir. He was, in fact, refused admittance!

The position had now become very strained. Lord Lytton had to consider that the mountainous region covering the north-western frontier of the empire of which he was Viceroy, a region upon the maintenance of which the predecessors of the English, the Mogols, had always insisted, which covers all the passes through which invaders of India have passed and must pass, and the possession of which by Russia would leave India at the mercy of Russia, was now held by an Amir who, spurning his offers, had consented to be the vassal of Russia. He had to consider that every move of the Amir, his hostile attitude, his refusal to receive his envoy, had been dictated by the Russian guests whom he was entertaining at his capital, and that these might at any moment suggest action which would for ever paralyze British interests. There was a strong Russian force at Samarkhand, and there were detachments between that city and Kábul. If these were to be called up, the situation would become extremely perilous.

Reluctant, however, to proceed to extremities, Lord Lytton resolved to afford the Amir one more opportunity to return to a better mind. He wrote to him, then, to the effect that a marked insult had been offered to the envoy whom he had ordered to proceed on a complimentary visit to his capital; that he trusted the Amir would, upon reflection, realize that such action was not in accordance with friendly relations between two neighbouring nations: that, if deliberately intended, it was a hostile act; but that in the hope that it was not deliberately intended the Viceroy was glad to give the Amir the opportunity of disavowing it, or, if it had been done by his express orders, of now expressing his regret for the same. Lord Lytton added, that unless a satisfactory reply were received before the 20th November he should be forced to regard the insult as deliberate and intentional, and that he should treat the Amir as an enemy.

The date, the 20th November, fixed for the receipt of the reply, allowed the Amir six clear days to consider his position. On the 19th he penned a reply—a reply as evasive and unsatisfactory as the communication he had received in 1873 from Lord Northbrook. This reply did not however reach the Viceroy till many days after the date he had mentioned. On that date hostilities had commenced.

Such was the origin of the second Afghán war. A hard and unelastic principle of policy, the principle thoroughly expressed in the words "masterly inactivity" applied to it by its authors, designed in its origin to deal with an Afghánistán bounded on the north and north-west by wild and independent tribes, had been rigorously applied to an Afghánistán watching with beating heart the steady absorption of those independent tribes by the great Northern Power which since 1859 had been no longer held back by the barriers of the Caucasus. In her fear and her agony Afghánistán had appealed to the Power of which she herself constituted the outer bulwark—she had appealed to the British rulers of Hindustán. In her appeal to those rulers she pointed to the fact that one kingdom on her north-eastern border had been virtually swallowed up; that but one month had elapsed since another kingdom, beyond her north-western frontier, had been suddenly and without warning annexed; that she was now threatened; and she asked alike for sympathy and assistance. Both were refused. An empire might be lost, but the principle of a hallowed phrase was not to be infringed. The rulers of England, but just awakening to the conviction that, in the matter of Khiva, they had been deliberately tricked and deceived by Russia, professed their willingness to be deceived once again, to believe pledges made only to be broken, to trust in promises which were violated before the paper had absorbed the ink with which they were written. They answered then the entreaties of Afghánistán with a complacent assurance that they did not share her alarm; that, if she were attacked by Russia, and if, then, the negotiators of England failed to induce that power to desist, it was "probable" that they would assist Afghánistán with troops, provided always it were made clear to them that her ruler would follow their advice and that Afghánistán "had abstained from aggression"! Well might the Amir remark "the goat attacks not the panther;" well might he declare his determination to receive no more favours from the English! Can we wonder that, baffled in his hopes, as he knew himself to be, fooled, as he believed himself to be, he should take an early opportunity to defy his former protector, and throw himself into the arms of England's enemy? Between two colossal powers, one of whom was profuse of promises, the other cold and unsympathetic, it was surely natural that he should prefer the former!

The second Afghán war, then, was the natural outcome of the repellant policy of 1873. It devolved upon Lord Lytton to carry it out. He had a great opportunity. In the Indian army he possessed, in 1878, an unsurpassed material, and he was gifted with the power of taking accurate stock of the men with whom he was brought into contact. It was the perception of Lord Lytton that gave to Sir Frederick Roberts the opportunity which brought him speedily to the very foremost rank. Side by side with Roberts were such men as Charles MacGregor, Donald Stewart, James Hills, not to speak—for the list is a long one—of very many others. The Sikh and Gúrkah regiments were well-drilled and disciplined and eager for a forward movement. The cavalry, the artillery, the commissariat, were thoroughly organized and ready for the campaign. Whilst Lord Lytton, then, had a splendid opportunity, he possessed ample means for using that opportunity, for settling for ever the Russo-Afghan question. That he did not settle it is clear. How was it then that he failed?

The fault was not the fault of Lord Lytton. In the part which devolved upon him he had done all that was possible. He had chosen the right men and supplied them with the best materials. A civilian, even though he were Viceroy, could do no more. The results justified his anticipations. The second Afghan war had begun the 20th of November, 1878. In May of the year following Yakúb Khán, son and successor of Amir Sher Ali, who had died, entered the British camp a supplicant for peace!

That event gave the British Government the long-desired opportunity. In a speech made at the Lord Mayor's banquet in November 1878, Lord Beaconsfield had declared that the main object of the armed intervention in Afghánistán was to obtain "a scientific frontier." Like all the phrases used by that distinguished statesman when he wished to emphasise a particular line of action, the phrase caught the public ear and was repeated all over the country. Not every one, however, asked himself or cared to ask others what it really meant. The phrase was so sonorous and expressive that the general public was content to accept it without inquiry.

There were, however, some who examined more closely its real meaning. Amongst these was the gallant soldier and distinguished strategist from whose lecture in 1884 I have quoted in a previous chapter, Lieutenant-General Sir Edward Hamley.

To Sir Edward Hamley the phrase could have but one significance. To him a scientific frontier meant a strategical frontier—a frontier, which, making India safe against every chance of invasion, should allow the races behind it's line to live undisturbed by continual scares. Was such a frontier possible for India? To give an answer to that question Hamley applied to the study of the subject a mind singularly clear and well-stored. When he had thoroughly mastered it, he, in response to a request made to him by the Council of the Royal United Service Institution, delivered his views on the 13th of December, 1878, to a large and distinguished audience assembled in its theatre.

Never did Sir E. Hamley more completely vindicate his title to the character of strategist than on this memorable occasion. He depicted, with a master's hand, the conditions of the Indian frontier; showed that the line of the Indus was no real barrier against invasion; that, if proper precautions were taken on the Pesháwar plain, we need not be apprehensive regarding an invasion through the Khaibar pass; that neither the Khuram Pass, nor the Gomal, need inspire us with serious alarm; but that between Kandahar and the Indus were plains of remarkable fertility which could subsist an enemy's army until its general should choose the opportune moment and the easiest point when and where to cross the Indus. He came to the definite conclusion, then, that we should occupy the salient angle which covered that country and all the passes leading into India behind it. That salient angle was represented by Kandahar. "I have endeavoured," said Sir Edward, in concluding a lecture which will prove to after ages that there was at least one English soldier who thoroughly understood the position, "to sketch a definite plan upon which to concentrate our resources, and by which to secure a scientific frontier, and a permanent settlement of this large question. Looking at the northern half of this part of our territory, I think we should be thankful for possessing a frontier so easily rendered impregnable. Looking at the southern half, we have no less reason to be thankful for having acquired, in Quetta, such means of vigorous and effective action, and such an opportunity of securing new advantages of the most important and decisive kind. With a garrison strongly posted in its lines at Kandahar, with all the routes and stages by which our forces might be assembled on that point, all sources of supply, and all arrangements for transport, laid down, as our trained staff officers are certainly capable of laying them down, we might view calmly any possible complications before us, whether arising from the augmented military power of Russia in the East, from the success of her intrigues, or from her open hostility. The grounds of our assurance would be manifest and easily understood, our native subjects would soon learn to appreciate them, and what would be security for us would be tranquillity for India."

Speaking on the same subject, two years later, at the *Royal Geographical* Society, an officer of Engineers, distinguished for his attainments and who had visited the country, thus supported Sir E. Hamley's view :—

"From a commercial, political, or military point of view," said Captain Holdich, "Kandahar is the most important point in Afghánistán; geographically it may be said to indicate the weak point of the Afghán frontier. There is no Hindu Kush between Kandahar and the north-west, nor is the distribution of the hill country round Kandahar of such a nature, or such an extent, as that which enabled the tribes of the north to make so formidable an opposition to us last winter.

"The broad open plains which surround Kandahar are not well suited to Afghán tactics. Whatever difficulty we may have in dealing with a foe whose strength lies chiefly in his power of scattering, or concentrating, as the case may be, by making use of mountain tracts and unknown hill paths, vanishes when the country becomes flat and open. To hold Kábul would mean to hold an extensive line of hills round Kábul. To hold Kandahar means very little more than retaining command of the walls and citadel. The chief wealth of Afghánistán too is certainly concentrated in Kandahar and Herát. Compared to Kandahar, Kábul is but an arsenal, and a convenient strategical point from which to govern the turbulent northern tribes. It is not a centre of trade in any sense, nor has it the command of such grand trade routes as Kandahar possesses. But Kandahar lies just as easily open to approach from one side as from another."

This, then, was the real scientific frontier—the extension of the British frontier to Kandahar, the annexation of the undulating Chatiali plateau behind Tal, and of the Pishin valley. The fortifications of Kandahar to be strengthened and that place united by rail with Girishk, Farah, and Herát, which last place should be placed virtually under British protection.

I have said "to Kandahar;" but the occupation of that town should include the occupation of the country as far as the Helmund. "When we speak," said Sir E. Hamley, on a subsequent occasion—

"Of occupying Kandahar, it is not merely the city that is meant. To hold a city against a besieger bringing modern artillery to bear on it, is to doom it to ruin, its inhabitants to destruction. Positions must be held at a distance—in this case up to the line of the Helmund. These positions, in order to draw from them their full advantage against such forces as the Russians could bring on us, should be carefully fortified with earthworks, and armed with artillery more powerful than could follow the march of an invader. Sir Michael Biddulph, in a valuable report made from personal observation during the last Afghan war, says, 'The position of Girishk is with the most modest precaution unassailable—all the passages of the Helmund can be defended by suitable works at short notice.' This being the first line, he describes a second strong line behind it—and a third, if necessary, is to be found, he says, on an arc extending from the edge of the desert. 'Inside this arc,' he goes on, 'lies all the productive country, while without it the country is sterile and an open glacis.' 'It seems to me,' he adds, 'that even though invasion may be remote, the possession of this point has an importance which cannot be rated too highly.' It is upon the Helmund, then, that we must direct our march, if we occupy Kandahar. And if we do not occupy it, we can never be certain that Russia will not anticipate us on the Helmund."

Now, when in May, 1879, Yakúb Khán entered the British camp at Gandamak to accept any terms which the British Government might offer, the obtaining of the strategical frontier described by Sir Edward Hamley was easy. We had but to ask for it to get it. That we did not obtain it was more the fault of the Ministry in Downing Street than of Lord Lytton.

If Lord Lytton had proposed such a frontier the Cabinet doubtless would have supported him. Lord Lytton did not propose it, because, being a civilian, he had to depend for his strategical plans on the military advisers at his elbow, and amongst those advisers there was not one who was possessed of practical strategic knowledge.

I do not refer to men like Roberts, MacGregor, Stewart, or Hills. They were with the army in the field. But, at Simla, Lord Lytton was surrounded by theorists, each of whom had his favourite plan—plans built not, as was Hamley's, upon knowledge and argument, but upon reasons which the supporter would have found it difficult to maintain before a critical assembly of experts. To put the matter tersely and clearly, it was Lord Lytton's painful task to have to select from a number of plans, all of them incongruous and defective, the plan which he deemed the least harmful.

It is possible—I do not know—but it is possible he may have been hampered by the Home Government. Certainly it was in the power of the Home Government either to force a plan upon him or reject and alter any which he might propose. Whether they did so or not I cannot say. At any rate they must bear the responsibility.

Now that the Cabinet which ruled the British empire between 1874 and 1880 had clear minds regarding the "scientific frontier" which its brilliant chief desired to secure it is impossible to assert. It is most painful to me to be obliged to admit that, not only had its members no clear views, but they had no definite ideas whatever on the subject. This was patent up to the last moment of their remaining in power. They adopted a right principle and an intelligent policy only from the moment when they were relegated to the cold shade of opposition.

Regarding "the scientific frontier," the Cabinet of 1879 had ideas, I have said, neither clear nor definite; and they had, moreover, no competent military adviser to inspire them. Not indeed, because there were not military advisers at their elbow. The lecture of Sir Edward Hamley had been delivered to a very distinguished and a very critical audience, had been spoken of on the very evening of its delivery in the House of Commons, had been noticed in the leading articles of our daily newspapers, and had attracted an extraordinary amount of attention. Wisdom had cried aloud in the streets, but the members of the Cabinet had shut their ears!

The fact is, that in all matters relating to the Afghan question the Cabinet of 1874–80 floundered from first to last. Succeeding a Cabinet which had adopted and persistently acted upon the fatal principle expressed by the words "masterly inactivity," the Cabinet of 1874 resembled, in its Indian policy, a man who knew that if he were to stand still he would die, but who was afraid to move forward lest he should stumble into a bog. And that expresses exactly what this Cabinet did do. Although Sir Edward Hamley held up a lantern to shew them the solid path along which they might tread with security, their fears whispered that the light of his lantern was the light of a will-o'-the-wisp : they took then a step in an opposite direction, and suffered the catastrophe I have mentioned.

For the "scientific frontier" obtained by the Treaty of Gandamak was, in very deed, the work of unscientific men. It was a delusion and a snare. It gave India a frontier a thousand times more unreliable than the frontier which it had abandoned to obtain it. It gave us the Khaibar Pass, when we were far better off in the valley of the Indus ready to receive an enemy emerging from that pass ; it gave us the Khurm valley, the occupation of which would have isolated a portion of our army : it's one solitary merit was the acquisition of the valley of Pishin.

It did not last long. We acquired it absolutely, that is, the treaty which gave it to us was ratified, the 30th May ; the gallant Cavagnari was murdered on the 4th September. Three months of existence were ample for so grotesque an abortion ! It's early death, followed though it was by a renewal of the war, was a blessing for which the authors of its existence ought to be for ever thankful !

Two days after the murder of Cavagnari, Roberts, the most brilliant, the most daring, the most accomplished of generals, commenced the war. Of such a man, of such men as Hamley, as Charles MacGregor, and as Hills, it is inspiring to write. But that task is now denied me. I have to deal only with the results of the campaign. It is however, at least satisfactory to know that such men still survive for the service of Great Britain.

The war thus re-commenced continued till the close of 1880. Eastern Afghánistán, or Kabulistán, had been evacuated the 11th August, and the rule over that portion of the country conferred upon Abdul Rahmán, the relative whom Sher Ali had defeated and driven into exile in January, 1869, and who had since that time been living in Bokhára, a pensioner of Russia. But in what is generally called western Afghánistán, that is, in the country about Kandahar and from Kandahar northwards the war continued some time longer. Holding, as I do, with General Hamley, that there was no necessity whatever to interfere in eastern Afghánistán; that the true interests of England were bound up in the line from Quetta to Kandahar and from Kandahar to Herát; that that is the line which, to bar Russian invasion, we have to occupy and secure, I shall confine my comments to the action of the British Government on that line.

The renewal of the war had given the Conservative Cabinet another chance. After the collapse of the Treaty of Gandamak, some dim light of the truth of Sir Edward Hamley's arguments would seem to have removed a portion of the fog which had obscured their reason. The apprehension stole upon them that the Kandahar line might, after all, be the true line. If we were to judge only from their after conduct when in opposition we might even believe that the apprehension grew into conviction. If that were so, they were more worthy of condemnation than if their vision had remained clouded. For this at least is certain, they never rose to the height of the situation. They showed themselves painfully wanting in accurate knowledge, in decision, in that quality which will cover a multitude of minor sins, in pluck. Having Kandahar in their possession, convinced as we must suppose they were convinced, of its enormous importance—for, subsequently, they all voted for Lord Lytton's motion for its retention, in the House of Lords, and for Mr. Stanhope's motion in the House of Commons (March, 1881)—they had not the courage to put their foot down and say "possessing this important place, this place so necessary to the safety of India, we will keep it." No—they adopted one of those half-measures which are the bane of true statesmanship—such a half-measure as the elder Pitt would have spurned and Palmerston would have derided—they placed there in supreme authority a cousin of the late Amir, a man likewise named Sher Ali, who under the name of "Wali" or more properly, "Vali," was to conduct the civil administration of the districts dependent upon the city. For all the good that this appointment caused, the Government might as well have stuck up a lay figure. The people in the country covered by Kandahar were longing for the British rule: they came in crowds to the political officer in charge of the Chatiáli district to implore it. A bold announcement that England had advanced her frontier as far as Kandahar would have had an immense influence for good. The appointment of the "Vali" shewed to the populations that there was still a chance of their being relegated to the hated rule of Kábul. Nor, whilst thus productive of evil, was the measure accompanied by any corresponding advantage. From first to last the "Váli" remained what I have said he might as well have been—a lay figure. On the first important disturbance, 14th July, 1880, his troops deserted and he collapsed, though he did not actually disappear till the following December!

The collapse of the "Vali" was a result second only, in the beneficial chances which it offered to Great Britain, to the disappearance of the treaty of Gandamak. Like that fortunate collapse, it gave England another chance to retrieve her political errors—to secure a really scientific frontier.

But, before that chance offered, a change had occurred in the guidance of the political destinies of Great Britain. The Ministry which had desired "a scientific frontier" had gone out, and the advocates of "masterly inactivity" had come in. The men who had composed the retiring Cabinet recovered their senses and their courage only with the first inhaling of the opposition breeze. It was, indeed, high time that they should recover both. If it be true, as was stated in January, 1880, and has been repeated without contradiction over and over again since that date, that in that month they were treating with Persia for the transfer to that power of the important city and district of Herat, they must have been absolutely on the verge of imbecility. Why, it was to prevent the consummation of such an event that Lord Palmerston planned the first Afghan war, and that he made war on Persia in 1856! And, in spite of that, a Conservative Ministry actually debated whether, to relieve themselves of responsibility, it were not advisable to do that which the greatest foreign minister—I might almost say, the only foreign minister—of this century had waged two wars to prevent! Did they ask themselves for a moment what such a transfer would mean; that the handing over of Herát to Persia would signify the handing over of Herát to Russia? If, in their forgetfulness or neglect of history, they had doubted then, can they doubt now? Does not the fate of old Sarakhs read a lesson? Has the occupation of Pul-i-Kishti and of the Zulfagar Pass, and the threat to occupy Panjdeh—places far beyond the frontier accepted by Russia in 1872 and never till now repudiated—not opened their eyes? Or, is it a fact, that if Russia were to occupy to-morrow the hill which is said to command Herát, a terrified English Ministry, and an ignorant and gullible British public would readily swallow the excuse that there was a new Herát as well as an old Herát, and that Russia had only taken the latter?

If the Conservative Cabinet had transferred Herát to Persia, they would have deserved impeachment. But the conduct of its members since they have been in opposition has been so much more bold and decided on all matters affecting the frontier policy of India that I am willing to hope, even to believe, that the idea, if seriously discussed at all, was discussed only to be dismissed. But, before I advert more fully to the true conception of the national interests which has guided them in opposition I must notice the action of their successors which caused it.

The Afghan war was still unfinished when the "masterly inactivity" party returned to power. To them it had been, and was, gall and wormwood. But the defeat at Maiwand and the subsequent leaguer of Kandahar by Ayub Khan had placed them in the, to them, extremely painful position of being forced to continue the war. From this painful position they were rescued by Sir Frederick Roberts, whose brilliant march and subsequent decisive victory will ever remain one of the most cherished records in the military history of Great Britain. This victory concluded the war.

Still Kandahar was in our hands, and we might easily have made it a condition with the new Amir whom we had placed in authority, that we should hold it. The reader must bear in mind that the question came up for the last time in the year 1880–1, at the time that Skobeleff was preparing the expedition which subdued the Akhal Turkomans. The idea then occurred to me that if those splendid warriors were subdued, and we should, in the very same year, evacuate the frontier fortress which covered all the western passes into Hindustan, the easily impressed peoples of India would not fail to imbibe the idea, not only that England was retiring before Russia, but that, from fear of Russia, she had left open the one gap in her frontier line, through which the invaders of India from the north had always advanced. To test the correctness of these ideas I visited India, and spent nearly three winter months there, from November to the third week of January, 1880-1. Thirty-five years of previous residence in all parts of the country had made me acquainted with most of its representative men, and I had little difficulty in inducing them to speak frankly with me on the subject.

I found, amongst all classes, among Muhammadans as well as among Hindus, a remarkable agreement of opinion. They all condemned the abandonment of Kandahar as likely to cause the people of India to lose confidence in the stability of British rule. "Nádir Sháh came by that route" they said, "and though Kandahar stopped him for a year, nothing stopped him after he had taken that place. Russia will of course conquer the Turkomans. And then Russia will be in the place of Nádir Sháh. If you leave Kandahar, you will leave open a gap by which Russia will easily enter. The native princes, men like Scindiah and Holkar, know that as well as you do. They bear your rule because if you were not here they would fight amongst themselves, and they know you can defend them and maintain order. But if they once think that a greater than you is coming, and they will think so if you deliberately leave the gate open for him to come, the hope of gaining something out of a general scrimmage will pervade their minds, and when you send your army to meet Russia on the Indus, they will strike for independence in your rear."

Such was the general opinion expressed to me by the Natives of India, who, in my judgment, were best capable of gauging the views of their countrymen. Shortly after my return to England I embodied, at the request of the members of the Constitutional Union, my experiences in the form of a lecture, which I delivered in February or March of 1881 to a large audience in St. James's Hall. I am bound to add that the Conservative party had long before become alive to the necessity, in the interests of the Empire, of retaining Kandahar as the new frontier. Lord Lytton had in the meanwhile returned home, and, I cannot doubt, had expressed very freely his views on the subject. This, at least, is certain, that the idea of the retention of Kandahar was adopted by the Conservative opposition, and was made the main theme of their platform speeches during the autumn of 1880, and the first ten weeks of 1881.

It soon transpired, however, that the Ministry of "masterly inactivity" had no idea of retaining the place. It is curious, looking back from the status of accomplished facts, writing in the third week of this month of March, 1885, when Russia possesses Sarakhs and Merv, and has advanced to Pul-i-Khátun and Zulfagar, within the Herát territory and within striking distance of the city of that name—it is curious, I say, to notice the reasons given by the authorities whom they quoted, upon which the Ministry relied to justify their retrograde movement. The most valued of these authorities, General Sir Henry Norman, arguing, in a memorandum dated 20th September, 1880, against the retention of Kandahar, thus expressed himself: "The *probability of our having to struggle for Herát*, or to defend India from Kandahar, is so remote that its possibility is hardly worth considering." Wonderful forecast! The time so remote as to be hardly worth considering has narrowed itself to a term of less than five years! Sir Evelyn Baring, another expert of the masterly inactivity school, was equally sceptical. Then there was the new Viceroy, Lord Ripon, whose experience of rather less than one year was so valuable: and, last not least, there was that eminent Russomane—the Prime Minister. "I have no fear myself," had said that high authority, on November 27, 1879, "of the territorial extensions of Russia, no fear of them whatever. I think such fears are only old women's fears." Possibly some of the constituents and many of the friends, perhaps even some of the colleagues of Mr. Gladstone, regard now that remark as a libel upon old women!

The question was debated in the House of Lords, on the motion of Lord Lytton, on the 5th March, 1881. There the motion for the retention of Kandahar was carried by a majority of 89 (165 against 76). In the House of Commons, after a debate of two nights, a similar motion was defeated (26th March) by a majority of 120 (336 against 216). Of the motives which influenced some at least of the members of that majority I have a word or two to say.

On the evening on which the division was to take place, the 26th March, I happened to be dining at a Club of which I am not a member. Before I sat down, my host informed me that a friend of his, a Liberal Member of Parliament, was very anxious to speak to me on the subject which was then engrossing the attention of the House, and that he would come over, if I did not mind, at 10 o'clock, for that purpose. I at once cordially assented. At 10 o'clock the member came over, was introduced to me, and began questioning me about Kandahar. After I had answered all his questions the Member thus addressed me:—"Colonel Malleson, I had previously read all you had written; I have now heard all you have to say on the subject of the abandonment of Kandahar: I have no hesitation in telling you that I agree with you to the fullest extent, absolutely and entirely: I am satisfied that if we abandon Kandahar we shall have to fight Russia on the frontier for our Indian empire, and it is quite upon the cards that we may be at the same time struggling with the native princes within its borders. Holding as I do these opinions, you will be surprised to hear that it is my intention to-night to vote for the abandonment of Kandahar!" Completely taken aback by this conclusion, so opposed to the preamble of the Member's speech, I could only exclaim:—"Good God, Sir, have you got a conscience?" The Member, in no way abashed by an exclamation which he probably expected, replied at once with a jaunty air:—"Conscience! Yes I have a conscience, and I'll tell you how it moves me to-night. Shortly after I had taken my seat for the first time in the House of Commons, a friend, who had been many years a member, came up to me, and congratulating me on being there, expressed a hope that I would keep my seat as many years as he had kept his: he added that I would keep it, too, if I would only adopt the plan which he had marked out for himself, and invariably followed. I asked my friend to tell me his plan. 'Why' he replied 'it is simply this. Never make a speech, never give a vote, in this House, without first asking yourself, on your conscience,'—mind you, he used the word conscience—'whether that speech or that vote will imperil your return at the next election.' Now," added the Member, "I have a very shrewd idea that if I were to vote in favour of the retention of Kandahar I should imperil my seat at the next election: therefore I am going down to vote against it. And I can tell you," he added, "there are at least fifty, probably seventy or eighty, members of our party who agree with me as to the necessity of retaining Kandahar, but who, actuated by the motives which actuate me, will vote for its abandonment."

Comment on this story is unnecessary. It is one of the saddest signs of the times that on questions affecting the welfare of Great Britain conscience is often dead!

Kandahar was abandoned. The very rails which the energy of Sir Richard Temple had collected near Sibi to continue the railway from Nari—just beyond Sibi—to Quetta and thence to Kandahàr were sold as old iron at a loss, according to the Blue Books, of more than half a million sterling!

But Time is rightly called the avenger. The news of the progress made by Russia along the northern frontier of Persian Khorásán induced even the representatives of the masterly inactivity party to repair some of the evil which had been effected. Quietly and uuostentatiously new rails were sent to Sibi, and large gangs were set to labour at the earth-way. It was resolved in fact to carry out the original plan of continuing the railway to Quetta, and, it is to be hoped, to Kandahar. Efforts were made similarly to induce the Amir, Abdul Rahman, to believe that the British were really his friends. He was assured, in terms far more positive and direct than those which were employed towards Sher Ali in 1873, that should Russia venture to invade his dominions he would receive strong and efficient support: that England recognized it as a duty devolving upon her to insist upon Russia adhering to her famous declaration in 1869, that "Afghánistán was completely without the sphere in which that power was called upon to exercise her influence." If England had at the same time put her foot down—if she had responded to the move of Russia upon Sarakhs by declaring that the crossing by that Power of the frontier line from that place by Robat-Abdullah Khan and above Andkhoi to Koja Saleh would mean war, we might have had no such disturbance as that which now exists. But once again was the Cabinet too soft. In reply to the plea of Russia that no proper frontier of the country comprised under the geographical term Afghánistán, existed, she agreed last year to despatch a Commission to mark out with precision, in conjunction with a Commission sent from Russia, the line which should thenceforward be recognized as the frontier across which Russia was not to advance. The line so marked was to be the dividing line between Trans-Caspian Russia and an Afghanistan subsidised by England.

CHAPTER VII.

RUSSIA'S LAST MOVE AND ENGLAND'S REPLY.

In justice, there should have been no question regarding the frontier of Afghánistán. I have already related that, when in 1869 Prince Gortschakoff informed Lord Granville that his master, the Czar, regarded Afghánistán as entirely without the sphere in which Russia would be called upon to exercise her influence, it was further agreed that all the countries in the effective possession of the Amír Sher Ali, and which had formerly recognized the sovereignty of Dost Muhammad, should be embraced under that name. Finally, after waiting for a report on the subject from General Kaufman which never came, Lord Granville wrote a despatch to Lord Augustus Loftus, in October, 1872, for communication to the Russian Government, in which he stated that not having received any letter on the subject from that Government, the Cabinet had decided to consider the undermentioned provinces as constituting the frontier provinces of Afghánistán :—(1) Badakhshán, with its dependent district of Vakhan, from the Sarikul (Wood's Lake) on the east, to the junction of the Kotcha river with the Oxus (or Peiya) forming the northern boundary of this Afghán province through its entire extent. (2) Afghán Turkistán, comprising the districts of Kunduz, Khulm, and Balkh, the northern boundary of which would be the line of the Oxus from the junction of the Kotcha river to the port of Khoja Saleh inclusive, on the high road from Bokhára to Balkh ; nothing to be claimed by the Amír on the left bank of the Oxus below Khoja Saleh. (3) The internal districts of Aksha, Seripul, Maimené, Shibberjan and Andkhoi, the latter of which would be the extreme Afghán frontier possession to the north-west, the desert beyond belonging to independent tribes of Turkomans. (4) The western Afghán frontier, a straight line from Khoja Saleh on the Oxus to Sarakhs on the Persian frontier. This line passed above Andkhoi and Gulu Bulu to Robat-Abdullah Khán on the Murgháb, thence by Imam Baksh to the Tejend, close to the town, on the other side of that river, of Sarakhs. Russia accepted that frontier in despatches dated respectively in December of that, and in January of the following, year. From that date to 1884, that frontier has never been questioned by that country. It has appeared on all the Russian maps. Even Schuyler speaks of it as well known and not needing further definition.

No questions, I repeat, were raised by Russia regarding this frontier till 1884. It was only when, in that year, the acquisition of Merv and Sarakhs brought her upon it that, in order to have a pretext for overleaping it, she suggested the proposal referred to in the last chapter. Russia would not have been true to her immemorial policy if, on approaching a new border, she had not at once raised doubts as to its validity. To solve those doubts, both countries engaged to send commissioners to the debated ground.

Though Russia agreed to this arrangement there are many reasons for believing that she did it solely to gain time, and with a determination not to act upon it. If she had any designs upon British India, the delineation of a frontier which she must respect would interfere very much with the use of those insidious means which had ever marked her stealthy progress. The sending troops across a frontier recognized by herself and guaranteed by England to the

Amír, would mean war with England as well as war with the Amír. She would be effectually prevented from justifying a forward spring by the use of such quibbles as she had employed regarding Sarakhs. At the same time she was not quite ready for war. Her Transcaspian railway, pushed on though it had been with the zeal of a Power which feels that it has a mission to fulfil, had not yet reached the required point. Other preparations were likewise not so forward as they might have been. Still she could not refuse to promise to co-operate in a plan so fair. We may fairly conclude from her subsequent conduct that she made that promise with a secret resolve to break it.

For, whilst Great Britain, true to her word, despatched, in the autumn of 1884, an English Commission, headed by an officer who had filled high positions in India; while that officer and his suite proceeded by way of Persia to the appointed place of rendezvous, Russia sent no one. For once, too, she had no excuses but the poorest to offer. Such as she did make reminded the British public of the taunting apologies suggested by the Prophet Elijah to the prophets of Baal for the absence of any manifestation on the part of their divinity. "Where is General Zelenoy?" asked the British public. "We do not quite know," answered Russia; "either he is talking, or he is pursuing, or he is on a journey, or peradventure he sleepeth and must be awakened." At all events he did not come to time.

Whilst the British Commissioner, Sir Peter Lumsden, and his escort, were waiting for his Russian colleague, General Zelenoy, the Russian commanders at Sarakhs and Merv determined to solve the question of the boundary by despatching small bodies of troops into the territory claimed and occupied by the Afgháns. If the reader will glance at any good map of the country immediately to the north-west of the Paropamisan range he will see marked, on the river Heri-rúd, at a point where the Keshef-rúd joins that river, the name of Pul-i-Khátun.* The Heri-rúd, whether under its own name or as the Tejend, constitutes to the south and to the north-west as far as Sarakhs the boundary of the province of Herát. The principal of the posts on its banks as it flows northward are Kuhsan, the Zulfagar pass, and Pul-i-Khátun. These posts have long been recognized as belonging to Herát. Yet, in a time of profound peace, whilst the British Commissioner appointed to mark out the boundary was waiting for his Russian colleague, Russian troops crossed the line then recognized as the boundary and seized a post, thirty-two miles to the south of it! Not content even with that they proceeded likewise to occupy the pass of Zulfagar, some twenty-eight miles still nearer to Herát!

There was no excuse for these acts: Pul-i-Khátun is merely a good place for a new departure; it is not even a village; it never belonged to, and has nothing in common with, the Turkomans, whether Sarik or other; it is simply an open ground covered to the east by high mountains. Of the ground immediately to the west of it Sir Charles MacGregor, who made the journey from Meshed to Sarakhs in 1875, gives the following account. I should premise that the road follows the Keshef-i Rud as far as Shor-jah, just beyond Ak-i-Durbend, and branches at a right angle northwards, just before reaching Pul-i-Khátun:†—"On

* Literally "The Lady's Bridge."

† To the number of the *Journal of the Royal Geographical Society*, for September, 1881, is attached an excellent map of this part of the country, of Northern Khorasán and the Kara-Kúm Desert, compiled from Colonel C. E. Stewart's survey of that country, from maps by Major the Hon. G. E. Napier, from the Surveyor-General of India's maps, and from the Russian Typographical Department of 1881. It is noteworthy *that, in all these maps, the Afghan frontier extends from Sarakhs, by way of Imam-Bakhsh and Robat-Abdullah Khán, in a straight line to a point above Andkhoi.*

Saturday the 24th of July, we marched 16 miles to Ak Durbend. The road leads down the valley almost the whole way, only occasionally leaving it to go over spurs to the left, which here and there impinge on the river. It is quite practicable everywhere for field artillery. At the eighth mile we passed a newly built fort called Bughbughoo, occupied by thirty wretched creatures, who looked at us passing with the longing of prisoners afforded a glimpse of the outer world.

"At the fourteenth mile we descended to the bed of the river and crossed to the right bank by a very nasty, because very muddy, ford. Thence the road went over an open plain for one mile, when it ascended over a spur by a steep, but otherwise easy pass, to another little opening, which was again divided from Ak Durbend by another similar pass.

"The river here is confined between hills, so that the valley is not more than 300 yards across, and beyond this it gradually gets narrower and narrower, till it becomes a regular defile, and continues thus till it emerges from the hills at Pul-i-Khátun where the ground becomes much more open. All access from the east is closed by towers placed on commanding positions overhanging the defile, so that the position of Ak Durbend becomes one of very considerable importance in considering the defence of this border, as by it is the only practical road between Múzduran and the southern side of the ridges which bound the Ab-i-Meshed on the south."

Four miles beyond Ak Durbend is Shorjah, where, as stated, the road branches northwards to Sarakhs. Pul-i-Khátun is about eight miles to the east by south from Shorjah. In his book (Journey through Khorásán in 1875) MacGregor gives sketches of Ak Durbend and of the gorge of the Ab-i-Meshed above Pul-i-Khátun.

On the subject of the sudden sweep of Russia upon that post, Professor Vambéry thus writes (March 1885)* :—"To this fact I reckon," that is, to the fact that Russia has a settled design to annex Herát, "before all, that lawless and unjust aggression of Russia on the north-eastern frontiers of Persia, an appropriation of a large tract of country to the occupation of which the Government of the Sháh has not given its consent, and the annexation of which has been only made with the obvious purpose to approach the district of Herát and to swoop down upon this important place in order to seize the Key of India, and so become the undisputable master of the country lying between the Paropamisus and the Oxus. I fully admit, as I stated in my previous paper on the Russo-Afghán Boundary Commission, that the country extending between the middle course of the Heri-rúd and the Murgháb, respectively, the Kushk (*rectius* Khushk = dry) river has formed, in the course of the present century, a debatable ground between Afghánistán and Persia, but since the last-named country was unable to clear this highway of the Turkoman Alamans (forays) on their inroads into the eastern part of Khorásán and Sëistan, the *de facto* possession must be, and can be, only accorded to the Afgháns, as to the Power able to put a check on the devastating incourse of the reckless freebooters of the north. If Russia had the sincere intention not to meddle with Herát, as her statesmen assert, the encroachment upon Sarakhs, whether the new or the old one, which is almost the same, would have been quite superfluous, and she could have easily avoided to rouse the just suspicion of England. But we see that quite the contrary has happened. Encouraged by the vague threats coming from the unofficial quarters of London and Cal-

* *Army and Navy Magazine*, April, 1885.

cutta, Russia hurriedly fell down still further to the south, and laid hand upon Pul-i-Khatún (the Lady's Bridge), at the very moment when the English Boundary Commission, headed by Sir Peter Lumsden, arrived at the spot. The object in view was to prove to the English that the place where the Keshef-rúd joins the Heri-rúd is Russian territory, and cannot be made the object of further discussion. But we beg leave to ask what are the reasons which have necessitated this step? There are no Turkomans subject to Russia in this outlying district, there is no interest to defend, and the whole movement is nothing else but a badly-concealed attempt against Herát."

The Zulfagar Pass is even stronger for aggressive purposes: I shall speak at greater length of this further on.

Writing on the subject from Bála Murgháb, forty-six miles below Panjdeh, the correspondent of the *Times* (March 12, 1885) writes as follows:—"You will see from the map that both the roads to Herát run through Badghis," the districts to the north and north-west of the city of Herát, "which comprises the valleys of the Heri-rúd, Kushk, and Murgháb. That is why it is so valuable to us and to Russia. If Russia had no designs on Herát she would not care whether her frontier were at Sarakhs or Pul-i-Khátun, or at Yolatan or Panjdeh. But of course she cares. Russia has statesmen, and each naturally aspires to be the Joshua who will terminate these weary wanderings and lead her armies into the Promised Land. Once there, their troubles are at an end. Everything is there to be found, for the valley of Herát flows with milk and honey." The writer closes a very interesting letter with the following pregnant sentence:—"*The two thousand miles we have marched between the Caspian and the Indus have certainly convinced us that India is the garden of Asia, and that only in India—Herát and Badghis are but oases—are water and shade the rule and not the exception. Now we can understand why there have been so many invasions of Hindustan."*

On the same point a well-informed writer in the same paper thus recently expressed himself :—

"At the time of the Russian war with Khiva, Sher Ali represented to the Viceroy his apprehension of the consequences that would ensue if the Turkomans of Merv were driven by Russian invasion into his province of Badghis. The fact that no European traveller passed through this region after Vambéry in the early days of Sher Ali's authority to tell us what the exact condition of Panjdeh was, is not an argument invalidating the Afghán claims over the place, especially as those claims are supported by the receipts of tribute from the surrounding tribes contained in the registers of the Herát Administration. If the presence of the Amír's troops and officials were to be made the only test of his right to rule there are many other places besides those which Russia has seized that Abdurrahman would have to surrender. It is, of course, intelligible that Russia should seek to make the Amír's burden in governing his state as heavy as possible, but it is difficult to understand how this argument can be indorsed by any impartial witness. The Amír holds Panjdeh, partly because it has always been dependent on Herát, and partly because he found it marked on the map well within the frontier drawn by the English Intelligence Department. But his chief reason of all is that the possession of Panjdeh is necessary to the preservation of his hold on the road running northwards from Herát through the province of Afghán Turkistan to Maimené and Balkh. Russia would give him that road and no more. It is absolutely essential to its security that the Ameer should retain the control of the region on its western flank, which includes Panjdeh and the Kushk valley. On the question of Panjdeh, as on that of Zulfagar and the Robat Pass, there is no room for discussion or difference of opinion. Those places form an integral part of the Amír's dominions, and apart from their own inherent value they are most important as constituting the natural out-works of Herát. The Russian troops have not yet assailed either Panjdeh or Khombou, but they are encamped close to the former place and at Zulfagar. We have frequently pointed out the risk thus created of a hostile collision, and we can only repeat, that an attack on either of these places could only be regarded as an act of unprovoked aggression upon the Amír which we should be bound to promptly resent by force of arms.

"Those persons who extenuate the latest phase of Russian aggression ignore all the circumstances which induced the English Government to join with Russia in an attempt to delimit the Afghán frontier. They purposely overlook the fact that the delimitation of the Amír's boundary on the north-west was taken up because Russia, only twelve months ago, seized Merv in supreme indifference to her repeated declarations to us that she had not the least intention of appropriating the Tekke stronghold. We have no wish to embitter the present controversy by dwelling upon past breaches of faith, but the sudden and secret occupation of Merv was an act that showed how illusory Russian pledges are. Yet now that Russia, far from standing still, has within the last year pushed her outposts 150 miles south of Merv, and to places within Afghánistán, we are again asked to confide to her honour when she repudiates all intention of treating Herát as she has treated the other places on the Murgháb and Heri-rud. When Russian troops entered Merv it was at once pointed out in these columns that the time had come for a definite and decisive policy with regard to the Russian advance towards India. We only acquiesced in the seizure of Merv on the express understanding that the frontier of Afghánistán should be clearly marked out, and that the least infraction of this line would be regarded by England as a *casus belli.* That course was adopted by our Government, and to all appearance that of the Czar also coincided in its justice and agreed to participate in giving it validity. To the policy of maintaining the integrity of Afghánistán this country was committed, not only by a sense of its own interests, but also by the definite assurances given to the Amír from time to time, and particularly in 1883. It is one from which the Government have as yet shown no sign of departing, and, indeed, the least symptom of wavering would be attended with fatal results to their own existence. They have from every point of view a position which is practically unassailable, so far as the matter is one of negotiation. The exchange of opinions which took place in 1872–3 between the two Governments on the subject of the Afghán frontier has been described as no longer binding on Russia; but the Russian Ambassador at the Court of St. James's was instructed in the spring of 1882 to state that the St. Petersburg Foreign Office still recognized the validity of the arrangement then concluded. This statement acquired more explicit value from being followed up by the declaration of Russia's readiness to delimit the Afghán frontier from the Oxus to Sarakhs. How, it may be asked, can Russia carry out her own proposition by throwing a loose line round the Salar and Sarik districts, and incorporating all the region up to the Paropamisus? The Russian acts now are in flat contradiction of everything stated by M. de Giers up to the period of the Merv occupation, and there is every reason to say that those expressions were repeated still more emphatically after that event had taken place.

"While the English Government are tied down to a policy of maintaining the integrity of Afghánistán by their formal representations to Russia and by their solemn pledges to the Ameer, the Russian Government equally bound themselves to co-operate in the task of delimiting 'the Afghan frontier from Khojah Saleh to Sarakhs.' In measuring the extent of the unfriendly action to which Russia has resorted within the last two or three months it is necessary to remember that the Frontier Commission was devised as a means of showing Russia's good faith, and of proving that the Czar's conquest of Merv did not constitute a menace to England, as many persons represented that it would. Nor can we lose sight of the fact that long before General Lumsden left London the scope of his labours had been defined by the highest Russian as well as English authorities. He was to complete what had been left unfinished in 1873, and to give the Ameer's territory, which was admitted to be 'outside the sphere of Russia's influence,' a recognized boundary from the Oxus to Sarakhs. It is as impossible to reconcile Russia's recent action with the original understanding regarding the labours of this Commission, as it is to discover in the occupation of Zulfagar and Pul-i-Khisti the evidence that the Russian Government has no sinister designs upon Herát and other places nearer India. Instead of cordially co-operating with us, as originally arranged, the Russian Government have delayed their Commission until their troops had occupied the most important positions within the debatable ground, and then they have brought forward the ethnographical principle, which should have been ventilated at a much earlier stage of the question if it was to be employed at all. Although they went so far as to nominate a chief Commissioner in the person of General Zelenoy last September, they have allowed him to remain ever since on his private estate near Tiflis; and when the season approached for beginning work on the spot, instead of hastening the movements of their representatives they sent an agent, M. Lessar, to London to make demands which are simply preposterous and to which no Government could venture to yield. In short, they have striven throughout to hoodwink our Ministers and to mislead English opinion; but they have already imposed more than enough on our credulity. Not only have they committed a flagrant breach of diplomatic etiquette, but they have really invaded Afghánistán. Unless they retire from the positions, which they should never have entered, there is little chance of averting a hostile collision, for the English Government can never concur in the violent seizure of districts to which Russia has not the shadow of a claim, and some of which are vitally necessary to the preservation of the Amír's authority in his kingdom."

Deferring to another chapter the consideration of the several routes from the important centre of Herát to the places on its frontier—for the districts in dispute must be regarded as outlying districts of the Herát province—I propose to treat now of those districts only, to seize which, Russia, in a time of profound tranquillity, and at the moment she had herself selected for amicable delineation, has violated the rights of nations and threatened the peace of the world.

The outlying districts comprise the territory comprehended between the line already marked from Sarakhs to Khoja Saleh, and an imaginary line below it, stretching from a point below the Zulfagar pass, sixty miles below Sarakhs, on the one side, between Panjdeh and Meruchak on the Murgháb, to a point just above Andkhoi, and thence by the existing line to Khoja Saleh. This line would bring Russia within easy striking distance of Herát!

If the reader will consult Colonel Stewart's map he will see that the first line, from Sarakhs to Khoja Saleh, cuts off the edge of the Kara-Kúm desert some distance above Gul-Bulu and a small portion of the same desert in the vicinity of Sarakhs. With these exceptions the district consists of valley, plain, and mountain, capable of being developed into an extraordinary state of fertility. To the west, from Sarakhs down to Kuhsan, up the Heri-rúd or Tejend, the country has never been occupied by the Turkomans, but that migratory tribes of that race have settled for a time in other parts has been a consequence of the generally disturbed state of the country. Turkomans were encamped for instance, at Panjdeh, when Captain Abbott visited that place in 1840. But the Turkomans who have occupied parts of those districts have been ever ready to submit to the prince ruling at Herát whenever he might show any disposition to enforce his power. They submitted to Sher Ali, and, as the reader will see from a letter quoted in the next chapter, no one has made a greater impression on the several tribes within his territories than the present Afghán ruler. If, then, the Russians should base their claims to the positions they demand on the Heri-rúd (Tejend) and the Murgháb, and the country above the imaginary line I have referred to, on the ground that, having occupied Sarakhs and conquered Merv they are the inheritors of the territories occupied by the Sarik Turkomans, those claims fall at once to the ground, for, whilst the positions on the Heri-rúd (Tejend) never were occupied by the Turkomans; whilst at the several points below Sarakhs villages were not built because of the dread of the Turkomans felt by the people; the tribes of that race who pitched their tents in the valley of the Murgháb, at Robat-Abdullah Khán, and below it, have, since 1863, and even previously, paid tribute to the representative of the Amír who was ruling at Herát!

But Russia wants that broad strip of land, first, because, situate for the most part below the desert, it partakes the general fertility of the Herát province, and may therefore be occupied as a base for operations against the valleys of Kushkh and Kala-i-nau. What those valleys are, what the country knows under the generic term "Hérat" is, will be explained in the next chapter. Russia wants that strip, secondly, because the possession of it will bring her within easy striking distance of the city of Herát; she wants it, thirdly, because, by taking it, she will absolutely neutralize Persia, by thrusting a wedge between the Persian town, Meshed, and her frontier.

Now, if we allow Russia to occupy these districts, or any portion of them, we virtually make her a present of Herát; and I raise again my warning voice to declare, that if Russia once be allowed to occupy Herát, the conquest of India by her will be a mere question of time. Even at Sarakhs, she was within 202 miles of the city of that name, whilst the English outposts are 514 miles distant from it, and 145 miles even from Kandahar. Since, then, she has illegally, against the law of nations, pushed her troops across the line, which, since 1872–3, has been recognized as the frontier line of western Afghánistán, and has occupied the pass of Zulfagar on the Heri-rúd, and the posts of Nikalshemi, Ak Robat, and Pul-i-Khisti, it is the duty of the Government of England to insist that she withdraw without delay. The insistance might be made now with effect, for the Transcaspian line of railway is not yet ready, and Russia is not, therefore, prepared for a mortal struggle.

Of the Russian claim to Panjdeh, a foreigner well competent to judge, Professor Vambéry, of the University of Buda-Pesth, writes as follows. Continuing the remarks which I have already extracted, about Pul-i-Khátun, he adds:

"Of a similar nature is the aggression planned, but hitherto frustrated, against Panjdeh (five villages), on the right bank of the Murgháb, there where the dreary sands of the Kara-Kum steppe ends and the cultivable country of the outskirts of the Paropamisus begins. In former times Panjdeh was a most flourishing place in the district of Herát, and under the reign of Sultan Husein Mirza Baikara, when the capital on the Heri-rúd was the cultural centre of the Eastern Mohammedan world, the environs of Panjdeh and Maruchak (Little Merv) were the favourite summer abode of the rich and luxurious world of Herát. In the subsequent periods we only occasionally meet with the name of Panjdeh in the historical works referring to this part of Khorasán, but we can safely assume that the ultimate destruction and desolation of the place dates only from the time when the Sarik Turkomans, vanquished by the Tekke Turkomans, had to retire towards the mountains, particularly to the region of Upper Murgháb, which was reckoned from immemorial times as belonging to Herát, and, since this place was taken by the Afgháns, as an integral part of Afghánistán.

"The Russian claim on this place is, therefore, from every point of view, unfounded and unjust. By their assertion that the Sariks have voluntarily acknowledged the supremacy of the Czar, they might claim the country on both banks of the Murgháb from Yolatan (*rectius* Yul-o-tin=passage) to Sari Yar and Ak Tepé, but not the country near and around Panjdeh, the Afghán property of which had been ascertained by the Russian traveller, Dr. Regel, in July 1884, who found there an Afghán garrison of a very unfriendly behaviour, in consequence of which he was obliged to change his route and to return, *viâ* Merv, to the Oxus.

Panjdeh, which the Russian traveller erroneously calls *Pandi*, is, therefore, in the unquestionable possession of Afghánistán, and the recent attempt of General Alikhanoff to overrun this place and lay hold on it in the name of the Emperor of Russia cannot be otherwise styled than an irruption into a foreign country, nay, into the dominions of a prince subsidized by England, consequently into the territory of a friend and ally of Great Britain."*

Subsequently, the 15th March, the same high authority wrote a letter to the *Times* (21st March), which virtually disposes of the assertion made by Russian partisans that Panjdeh had never previously been occupied by the Afghans, and was only recently taken possession of on the instigation of Sir Peter Lumsden. The letter runs as follows :—

"In your article entitled 'The question at issue between England and Russia,' published in the *Times* of the 13th instant, I read that the assertion of several leading German papers concerning the quite recent Afghán occupation of Panjdeh can be easily refuted by the fact that Abdurrahman had already ordered his troops to take possession of Panjdeh twelve months ago. In order to prove this fact your contributor proceeds to quote the events of 1883, when the ruler of Kábul got an English map showing the frontiers of his country towards the north-west, and it was in consequence of this cartographic communication that he found it practicable to put a garrison in the above-mentioned place on the Murgháb.

"As Continental critics may be rather sceptical as to English maps and English official communications, I beg leave to call your attention to a German scientific paper written by a Russian officer, in which it is clearly stated

* *Army and Navy Magazine*, April, 1885.

that Panjdeh was already in the possession of the Afgháns in June, 1884, and that it was not at all the instigation of the English, under Sir Peter Lumsden, which prompted the Afgháns to occupy Panjdeh and to provoke the quarrel between England and Russia in Central Asia, as Russian, German, and also French papers choose to imagine and to represent.

"The paper named is nothing else than the highly respectable geographical periodical known as 'Dr. A. Petermann's Mittheilungen,' volume 31, 1885, No. I., in which there is a notice by Dr. Regel, the explorer of Darwaz, Roshau, &c., concerning his journey from Tchihardjui across Merv to Pandi (Panjdeh) and back, executed in June, 1884, and where we read, p. 24—'Als wir am vierten Tage (*i.e.*, the 9th of June, 1884) auf Pändi (Pandjeh) losgehen wollten, brachten die Leute aus Yulitan (Yolöten) die Nachricht erstere Ortschaft (viz., Panjdeh) sei eben erst von 4,000 bis 5,000 Afghánen besetzt worden.'* There are other similar statements concerning the presence of the Afgháns in Panjdeh in the month of June, 1884, and as this German-Russian officer will not be suspected of prevalent English sympathies, and as he had written his paper long before the outbreak of the present quarrel, I venture to say the question of English instigation may be easily dismissed, as the testimony of the traveller named will suffice to refute any contrary statement."

It is clear, then, that against right, in the face of right, in defiance of her repeated protestations, Russia has crossed the border line which she agreed to in 1872-3, which is

* "When on the fourth day (June 9, 1884) we were about to proceed to Pandi (Panjdeh), the people from Yulitan (Yolöten) brought us the news that that place (viz. Panjdeh) had been but just occupied by from four to five thousand Afghans."

recognized as the border line in all the Russian maps of any authority. She has committed this infraction of public law at the very time she had herself selected for a new and peaceful demarcation of the frontier line, when she knew that a large English army and a contingent of Indian troops were in the Soudan, that the minds of the English ministers were occupied by grave European complications, and that England was less prepared for a great war than she had been for thirty years. She committed this infraction of public law, moreover, at a period when the counsels of England were guided by a ministry whom she had often deceived, and had found no difficulty in deceiving again: a ministry which she had seen yielding to bold deeds in the Transvaal, to pressure from France, to something very like menace from Germany: a ministry which had shown a strong inclination to undergo any humiliation rather than engage the country in war, even in rightful war. Feeling, then, as she had a right to feel, that the game of bluster and swagger was a safe game to play under the circumstances, she had played it boldly and unscrupulously. Pursuing the policy so aptly described by Lord Palmerston in his letter to Lord Clarendon, quoted in a previous page, she spoke in honied phrases at St. Petersburg, whilst, ready to disavow them if they should fail or to reward them if they should succeed, she instructed her agents on the frontier to strike the blow which might secure for her a new and very real base against India.

How have the Ministers of England replied to this audacious attempt? We all know how Mr. Pitt would have answered it, how Mr. Canning would have answered it, how Lord Palmerston would have answered it. We know how America, how Germany, how even France, would have met such an insult. Within four-and-twenty hours orders would have been transmitted from St. Petersburg to the frontier for the withdrawal of the Russian troops across the border. If the outrage had been met with firmness and resolution, prompt atonement would have been made. But, up to the present moment, our Ministers have displayed neither firmness nor resolution. Far from grasping the real significance of Russia's forward move, they have begun by making a concession which is a virtual yielding of Russia's demands. Russia had no case wherewith to support her impudent advance. Our Ministers have provided her with one. Let us imagine, if we can, a French army crossing the German frontier, which was finally settled about the same time as the Afghán frontier, and seizing Metz! Is it possible to imagine the German Chancellor allowing the invading army to remain in that fortress until it should be decided by negotiation to whom the line of the Rhine properly belonged: then to listen to Prince Bismark, when interrogated in Parliament, as he made a statement like the following?

"Upon that communication"—a demand by Prince Bismark for the withdrawal of the French troops—"a correspondence ensued, and the French declined to withdraw their troops. They gave certain explanations about them; and they founded their answer upon the belief they entertained that the territory is theirs, that they claim it as a matter of right. Well, sir, that being the state of the case—we of course had addressed a requisition to them in the belief that it was German territory—as the French made a serious claim to be the rightful possessors of the territory, we could do nothing in the matter consistently, I think, either with prudence or with any honourable regard to the interests of peace, except to prosecute measures for bringing about a proper investigation and decision of the claim that had been preferred. That being so, undoubtedly, I will not say actually, there has been a withdrawal of the requisition, but substantially it comes to the same thing. The application that was made has lapsed from the circumstances of the case."

And yet, *mutatis nominibus*, this was the precise explanation, these were the *ipsissima verba*, which the Prime Minister of England made when interrogated by Mr. Edward Stanhope as to the action he had taken with respect to the invasion of a frontier, which is, to all intents and purposes, the frontier of British India !

It is to a certain extent a satisfactory sign of the times that this reply of Mr. Gladstone has awakened the scorn and contempt of the men of all parties. The *Times* of the following morning expressed the general opinion when it lamented that the Prime Minister should have shown "so little of the spirit of a man who means to vindicate the rights of this country." . . . "To avoid war by simple abandonment of claims which have not been investigated by competent authority, and to permit Russia to retain positions which she has seized in defiance of her own admission of their doubtful ownership, is to proclaim ourselves impotent in presence of audacious aggression, and to deprive ourselves of the confidence which alone can lead to firm and fruitful alliance with Afghánistán."

It is in vain, I fear, notwithstanding this expression, and similar expressions, of opinion from all parts of the country, to hope that the Ministry will be inspired with the moral courage which can nip an evil in the bud. Too often have they turned their cheeks to the smiter. I would, however, ask them to remember that in this instance it is not a question of minor importance—it is an Empire which is at stake!

The rulers of England are the trustees for the people of England. I beseech, I implore them, not to neglect this opportunity of shutting the door to the invader. Let them "be just and fear not." If mistakes have been made by both parties in the past, let both unite in the sacred duty of firmly securing the noblest dependency of England. For it is that dependency, it is India, which is endangered by this advance. If my feeble voice cannot penetrate within the portals of Downing Street, if they refuse to hear me, let them listen to the voice of one to whom for many years they entrusted the Government of India, and to whose advice they are bound to pay attentlon. "My own view," wrote the Duke of Argyll, in a letter dated the 18th March of the current year, to the *St. James's Gazette*:—"My own view has always been that the conquest by Russia of the Tekke Turkomans and of all the khanates of Central Asia has been inevitable. I have held, further, that no civilization and no commerce could be established in those regions until that conquest had been accomplished; and that on this ground, as well as on several other grounds, it was at once useless and undignified on our part to be perpetually remonstrating against 'advances' which we could not prevent and which, in the interests of humanity, we ought not to regret.

"But none of these considerations apply to any advances by Russia across the borders of Afghánistán. We must insist on the independence and integrity of that country being respected; and in so far as the Afghán kingdom must of necessity be under any predominant influence, we must insist that this predominance shall be ours. I trust all parties are agreed in this doctrine and in this policy, and in desiring that our Government shall carry it into effect with firmness."

Finally, I would invite their attention to the remarks, published in the *Times* of the same date, 19th March, written by the great soldier whose warnings regarding the occurrence of certain events in Central Asia unless we should take certain precautions, have, unfortunately, always been neglected and always justified. "A very real danger has come," wrote Sir Edward Hamley, "without our seeking, to meet us on the Afghán frontier. It is impossible to conceal from ourselves the design with which Russia is pushing on. Our manner of meeting her is among the marvels of the most unaccountable period of our history. We treat her as one of two established coterminous Powers whose respective limits require definition. The facts are dropped out of sight that a few years ago she was a thousand miles from the Afghán frontier, that she grounds her brand new title to contest its territory with us on her conquest of certain predatory tribes on whose outskirts other predatory tribes wander, and that on the strength of this extraordinary claim she suddenly puts forth the impudent formula, 'Whatever territory you cannot satisfactorily prove your right to is mine,' which thenceforth becomes the basis of negotiation. What can such a pretension put in action mean but to defy us to war, with the alternative of ruinous submission? And, in fact, for weeks past, the daily question has been, 'Is there to be war with Russia?' an event only staved off thus far by the humiliating alternative. Like the terrified prey of brigands we have cast ourselves *ventre à terre*. But even submission the most abject cannot avail. The attitude we have chosen is not exactly the best for keeping the throat from the knife. And what effect will it have on our would-be allies, the Afgháns, the poverty of whose dialect does not perhaps enable them to discriminate nicely between an agreement and an arrangement! What effect, too, in India? If I do not speak of the effect in this country it is because we are, for the time, wrapt in an opium dream, in which facts count for nothing, delusions for much.

"By common consent, the reason for the Russian

advance is to be found in our embarrassments in Egypt. That being the case, what could Russia desire better if she herself had the ordering of our policy, than that we should cast fresh armies and new heaps of treasure into the Soudan? Can she be supposed to look on with other feelings than delight while British ships are landing railway plant by the hundred mile at Suakim? Had the same energy been displayed on the Indus we should now have had a railway to Quetta, perhaps to Kándahár, with ten thousand British troops at the end of it.

"What a sound judgment would seem to counsel, then, is an immediate reconsideration of our position. Nobody will maintain that we can carry on two wars, either of which would sufficiently tax our resources. We must choose between the will-o'-the-wisp and the mortal emergency. Happily, troops and material at Souakim are already so far on the direct way to Kurrachee. And for the force onthe Nile, if it can continue its retreat to Lower Egypt (and the doubt speaks much for the perverse ingenuity which created it), let it abandon its delightful and salubrious summer quarters and descend the river; thus, so many men will be saved towards the saving of the Empire. And let us simultaneously take all needful steps for placing an effective army in the field and putting this kingdom in a condition of defence. If, at the same time, that lost art, diplomacy, should chance to revive among us, it will find ample occupation in endeavouring to persuade the Afgháns to invite us to a military occupation of their country, in procuring friends among the European Powers, and in persuading the unspeakable Turk to form with us that agreement (or arrangement) necessary to enable us to operate effectively in the Black Sea."

These are pregnant words. Of this, at least, Englishmen

may be sure, that it is only by concentrating all the energies of Great Britain on the maintenance of the existing frontier of Afghánistán that Herát can be saved. If we allow Herát to fall, India is doomed. That the reader may understand this clearly I proceed to answer the query which I can imagine forming in his mind, "What are those places which thus seem to constitute the outlying redoubt of India?"

CHAPTER VIII.

THE OUTLYING REDOUBT OF INDIA.

THE city of Herát stands in the fertile valley of the Heri-rúd 2,650 feet above the level of the sea. The Heri-rúd rises in the mountains of Hazáreh, not far from the village of Robat Tarwan. Under the name of Jangal-áb it flows in a south-westerly direction to a point below Daolatzár, a village on the direct road between Herát and Bamian. At this point it is joined by another branch, the Sir Tingiláb, which rises likewise in the Hazáreh range, though at a point somewhat more to the south-east than the Jangal-áb. From the point of junction the united streams take the name of Heri-rúd and follow an almost direct westerly course south of the Paropamisan range. Some fifty miles beyond Herát, which lies near its northern bank, the Heri-rud takes a turn to the north-west and then to the north receiving many streams in its course and passes Rozanak, Kuhsan, Kasan, Pul-i-Khátun and Sarakhs. Between the two last named places it loses the name of Heri-rud and takes that of Tejend. Under this name it flows north-westward till it is lost in the sand and swamps of the great Turkoman desert.

At the point already indicated where the combined waters of the Sir Tingiláb and the Jangal-áb form the Heri-rúd, the river traverses a broad valley which it adorns and fertilises. All along this channels from the river spread over its broad surface, converting deserts into corn-fields, and waste lands into gardens of fruit. The supply from its swiftly running waters never fails. It was equal to the demand even in the days when Herát was the most famous city of Central Asia, possessing the most influential court and constituting the most splendid commercial mart in the Eastern world. Though the channels have been in many instances destroyed the supply is more than equal to the demand even now.

In this valley the city of Herát is the principal city. According to the graphic account of Conolly, who visited it in 1830, it is situated "at four miles distant from hills on the north, and twelve miles from those which run south of it. The space between the hills is one beautiful extent of little fortified villages, gardens, vineyards and cornfields, and this rich scene is brightened by many small streams of shining water, which cut the plain in all directions. A dam is thrown across the Heri-rúd, and its waters, being turned into many canals, are so conducted over the vale of Herát that every part of it is watered. Varieties of the most delicious fruit are grown in the valley, and they are sold cheaper even than at Meshed; the necessaries of life are plentiful and cheap, and the bread and water of Herát are proverbial for their excellence. I really never, in England even, tasted more delicious water than that of the Heri-rúd: it is 'as clear as tears,' and the natives say, only equalled by the waters of Kashmir, which make those who drink them beautiful."

The origin of the city can be traced far into antiquity. To the ancients the province of which it was and is the capital was known as Aria and Ariana. The city is mentioned by the earliest writers. Arrian writes of it as Artakoana or Artakána, the royal city of the inhabitants of Aria. It often served as the residence of the greatest conquerors of the East. Tradition brings to it Nebuchadnezzar and Semiramis. The Persian historians assert, with remarkable unanimity that Alexander the Great gave it the name under which Arrian writes of it. There can be no doubt but that the city was the gate through which the son of Philip of Macedon passed to the conquest of India.

It was towards the close of the tenth century that the valley of the Heri-rúd obtained the importance which it exercised during many centuries which followed. An oasis between the Turkoman deserts and the rocks and mountains of Afghánistán, the centre where converged the roads from Bokhára, from Persia, and from India, it became, at that period a commercial centre which even the contests between the Iránian and the Turanian did not disturb. In the year 1219 the city of Herát possessed 12,000 retail shops; 6,000 public baths, caravansaries, and water-mills; 350 schools and monastic institutions; 144,000 occupied houses; and the city was visited yearly by caravans from all parts of Asia.

The invasions of Chengiz Khan, 1219-22, and of Taimúr in 1381, inflicted upon Herát enormous damage. It was through her gates that the latter marched to the conquest of India. But the rebound was magical. Under the rule of Sháh Rokh, fourth son of Taimur, Herát soon vindicated her claim to the title of Queen of the cities of the East. The country beyond the Oxus boasted of many famous cities. There was Bokhára, and there was a city then more influential still, the famous Samarkhand. But Sháh-Rokh recognized in the province of Herát a military position whence he could hold fast the countries beyond the Oxus, whilst keeping in a firm grip the countries to the east, to the west, and to the south. Under his rule Herát became the capital of the whole of Central Asia.

The renewed prosperity of the city and province, beginning with the rule of the son of Taimur, 1396-7, lasted with but little interruption, to the period of its conquest by Persia in 1510. With that conquest the glory of the city departed. The monarchs of Persia neglected Herát to patronize a city of their own, the holy city of Meshed.

From the date of its capture by Persia, the province of Herát became the battle field between the Uzbeks and the Iránians. The city suffered many sieges. Finally it fell to the latter, and thence to the year 1715 it shared the fortunes of the Persian monarchy, neglected and all but forsaken, from that moment, until the death of Nádir Sháh.

It fell then into the hands of the Afgháns, and in their hands it has since remained.

The limits of the province of Herát have varied with the times. But regarding that province as constituting western Afghánistán it may be said to be bordered on the north by the line from Sarakhs to Khoja Saleh, on the west by the Heri-rúd, to the south-west by the Persian desert as far as Sëistan, to the south by the Heri-rúd; to the east by the mountainous ranges separating it from Andkhoi, Maimené and Shibbergan.

It's value to India rests on two facts:—the one patent to the eye, that as long as the province of Herát is held by an ally or dependant of the ruler of India, India is unassailable: the other that Herát constitutes a new and perfect base for a hostile army.

On the first point I would remark that Herát is called the gate of India because through it, and through it alone, can the valleys be entered which lead to the most valuable of all the divisions of Asia. Those valleys, running nearly north and south, are protected to the east by ranges practically inaccessible, to the west by sterile deserts. No invading army would attempt to traverse the great salt desert, and the desert immediately to the south of it, the Dasht-i-Naobad, whilst a British army should hold Herát. In the eloquent lecture, already alluded to, on the subject of the frontier of India, delivered by Sir E. Hamley in 1878, that master of the strategic art laid down the broad principle that if England were to hold the western line of communication with India, that by Herat and Kandahar, she need not trouble herself very much about the eastern or Kábul line. On the same occasion, the eminent soldier-politician who has made the question of the frontier policy of India the study of his life, declared, in reply to a question put to him, that rather than allow the occupation of Herát by Russia, he would venture the whole might of British India. Sir Henry Rawlinson saw clearly that the possession of Herát by Russia meant the possession not only of a strategic base whence Russia could invade India, but the possession of a country where she could remain quiescent until the opportune moment for making the fatal spring should arrive.

The mention of this consideration leads me to the second point of my argument—to the assertion that the province of Herát would form a secure and perfect base for an army of invasion. I have spoken of the wonderful fertility of the valley of the Heri-rúd. Ancient remains prove that the valley of the Murgháb has been and can be rendered again not less productive. The valleys of Khúshk and Kala-i-Nau, the country about Panjdeh, belong to the same category. Abbott, Conolly, Vambéry, found everywhere traces of large occupation. The province produces in abundance the willow and the poplar, trees which make the best charcoal. It possesses mines of lead, of iron, and of sulphur. The surface of many parts of the country is laden with saltpetre. Its fields produce in abundance corn and wine and oil. Place an army in the province which, called by its inhabitants Badghis, may be comprehended under the generic term Herát, and nothing need be brought to it from Europe. The valley which was the granary and the province which was the garden of Central Asia, can equip it, provide it with its *matériel*, ay, even with men and horses. On the city which gives its name to the valley, moreover, converge all the great roads, but one, leading on India. Occupied by Russia, it would become "an eye to see and an arm to strike."

These are not my words alone, they are not my thoughts alone. They are the words and the thoughts of every Englishman of ordinary intelligence who has studied the subject. They were the words and thoughts of the ever-to-be-lamented Bartle Frere: they are the words and thoughts of Hamley, of Rawlinson, of Napier of Magdala, of Roberts, of MacGregor. What says the latter, a most accomplished and instructed officer, on the subject? I cannot quote from the able memorandum which I received in confidence, but, fortunately, there is an appendix to his book on Khorásán which contains his views, written so far back as 1875, on the subject I am now discussing.

"It is not, however, sufficient," wrote Colonel MacGregor, "to show the importance of Merv. I will go further, and try and show why Herát is important, because of course if Herát were not important, and there was nothing beyond Merv but desert down to the sea, I need not have troubled myself to pen these remarks. Merv has almost no more value, apart from Herát, than the head of a sap has apart from a fortress selected for attack. I therefore wish particular attention to be given to the next step by which I hope to prove my case.

"Herát has been termed the Key of India, not lightly as a mere figure of speech, but by every officer who has had an opportunity of seeing its valley. It is so, because it is the nearest and best point at which an invader could concentrate and prepare for the invasion of that country; advantages which it gains from its beautiful valley, the fertility of which is unrivalled in Asia; from its strategical position, which gives it the command of all the important roads to India; from the great strength of its fortress, it being, in fact, the strongest place from the Caspian to the Indus; from its admirable climate, and from the prestige it enjoys throughout Asia.

"The fertility of its valley, and its capability of maintaining large forces, is proved by the fact that it has been besieged oftener than any city in Asia, and has always afforded supplies for the armies of both besiegers and besieged. And it must be remembered the first have sometimes reached as many as 80,000 men, and have seldom fallen below 30,000, while both have always been composed of undisciplined men who destroyed nearly as much as they consumed. Moreover, I have seen it with my own eyes, and I have no hesitation in saying that it is capable of maintaining a very large army.

"It will not be necessary to describe the defences of Herát, but only to remark that Sir H. Rawlinson's description is in no way exaggerated when he says, 'It is surrounded by works of the most colossal character, which, with the adaptations and improvements of modern science, might be rendered almost impregnable.'

"A glance at the map will convince any soldier of its importance strategically. No less than five distinct routes lead to Herát from the west, viz: 1. from Ashruff by Shahrood, Toorshez, Khaf; 2. from Guz by Bostam, Subzwar, Toorbut, Haiduree, and Shuhr-i-Now; 3. from Astrabad by Findurisk, Jahjurm, Jowen, Nishapoor, Furreeman, Shuhr-i-Now; 4. by the Goorgaun, Rabat Ishk, Boojnoord, Koochaun, to Mushudd, and Jam; 5. from the mouth of the Attruk, by that river through the same points. From the north two routes lead direct on to it from Merv, and a third arrives from Kirki by Maimené. Herát commands all these routes, as well as the routes to the south from Persia, viz. from Tún by Khaf, from Ghain, Subzwar, from Bisjund to Furrah, Herát and Lash. Moreover the routes leading out of Herát, or over which an army stationed here may be said to have the command are, 1. the route to Kábul by Bamian; 2. the route to the same plece by Behsood; 3. the same from Merv by Bala Murghab; 4. the route by Balkh to Kábul; 5 and 6. two routes to Kandahar; 7. the route to Ghuzni through the Hazarah country; 8. the routes from Persia which lead through Subzwar, Furrah, Lash or Sëistan, and which all converge on Kandahar.

"Besides all these positive and patent advantages which this place possesses, Russia in Herát would have an unassailable position, from which to threaten us in India, so as to force us to keep large forces always ready to meet the menace, while she would be able to cast abroad throughout India, that 'seething, festering mass of disaffection,' the seeds of a rebellion that would still further cripple us, she would altogether alienate from us the whole of the Afgháns, and the Persian Khorásánis, and would practically control for her own purposes nearly all their military resources."

In these remarks the whole case is contained. The conclusions, unfortunately, are irrefutable.

The principles which apply to the whole province apply equally to that northern portion of which is contained between the line of 1872 and the new line which the Russians are trying to enforce. The concession of that line would bring the Russian outposts to within a very short distance of Herát—not much greater than the distance between Dover and London. She would lie securely on two rivers, each possessing a full stream and an unsurpassed power of fertilizing—each, as I shall show in the next chapter, opening out a route easy to be traversed. In desiring to acquire these districts Russia can have but one object, and that object the one which has been the end and aim of her Transcaspian struggles. To allow her to retain the Zulfagar Pass, Pul-i-Khátun and Pul-i-Kishti, with the country to the north of these places, would be as criminal and as fatal to the nation allowing it, as if the commander of a fortress were to permit a hostile army to encamp on the glacis. The conquest of Merv and the occupation of Sarakhs brought Russia near enough to Herát—but little longer than the distance which separates the British outposts from Kandahar. If we would preserve Herát from her clutches, if we would maintain India, we are bound to insist that the border line from Sarakhs to Khoja Saleh shall be scrupulously respected.

CHAPTER VIII.

THE ROUTES ON THE FRONTIER.

I PROPOSE now to describe the routes, and with the routes the nature of the country, from Herát along the Heri-rúd to Sarakhs; from the same place by the Khushk river to its junction with the Murgháb; and from Herát, also, by the Kala-i-nau valley to the Murgháb. In carrying out this plan I shall make free extracts from the journals of older travellers, men such as James Abbott, Vambéry, Marsh and MacGregor, and contrast their experiences with those of the companions of Sir Peter Lumsden who have written on the subject to the London papers.

I take first the route from Herát to Sarakhs along the Heri-rúd valley, based upon the experiences of Captain Marsh, who traversed the country in 1872, and of Sir C. MacGregor who visited it the following year:

Riding westward the first stage lands the traveller at Ṣhakhwan a large group of three villages and a fort. The distance by the direct road is twenty-four miles, but to avoid the wet cultivation near the river it is often necessary to make a détour of eight miles, crossing the Julgha or plain of Herát "a sandy loam which bears good crops by irrigation."

The second journey is thirty-two miles to Sabash "a little, mean, dirty fort, barely habitable." The first part of the road takes the traveller along a network of canals as far as a ruined caravansarai; thence, along high grounds at some distance from the river to the fort of Rozanak, about four miles from the town of Ghorian to the south of it, and from Rozanak across a vast gravel plain with distant hills on both sides to Sabash.

From Sabash to Kuhsan the distance is but twelve miles across the same gravel plain. Kuhsan is now in ruins, but in Sir Charles Macgregor's opinion it could easily be improved "so as to make it worthy of the frontier fort of a warlike nation." The same authority speaks with enthusiasm of the fertility of its soil. "Conducted," he writes, "into a most delightful garden, I bivouacked under the shade of some fine plane trees, by a tank of delicious clear water. After a good bath in the latter, it was a great luxury to lie back in one's bed, and devour, for nothing, bunch after bunch of glorious grapes, that at home would have ruined me." He makes special mention of the splendid gardens and vineyards in the vicinity of the town, as well as of its windmills, which likewise are to be found in great abundance about Rozanak. Regarding its position MacGregor writes: "The position of Kuhsan is one of considerable importance as being the first village in the valley of the Heri-rúd which would be reached by forces coming from the west, and the point on which the roads from Tarbut, Meshed, and Sarakhs join. It is therefore a place where there should be a fort of considerable strength, because an invader could not venture to pass it without taking it, and if it were able to offer a respectable resistance, it would necessitate his being detained long enough among the barren tracts to the west."

The fourth day's journey is to Chasma-Saoz, a distance of twenty-four miles. The road, which is good, traverses a plain on the left bank of the Heri-rúd. Supplies of all sorts are here abundant. This journey terminates in a pass, which, judging from the equal distance, sixty miles from Sarakhs, can be no other than the Zulfagar Pass, recently seized by the Russians.

The fifth day takes the traveller to Pul-i-Khátun, twenty-eight miles. The road crosses the Kotal Ista-Khanchil pass, and then traverses hills, crossing to the right bank not far from Pul-i-Khátun. Though not good, it is practicable for guns. Not far from these hills, the most northern branch of the Heri-rud takes the name of the Tejend. There is no village at Pul-i-Khátun, but forage is abundant. The bridge which gives its name to the locality is an old bridge of stone.

From Pul-i-Khátun to Sarakhs, the distance is thirty-two miles, the road level all the way, over a plain on the left bank of the river. At sixteen miles the fort of Kala Daolatábád is passed; eight miles beyond, that of Naczabad.

Contrasting with this account is the graphic description of the same road, taken the reverse way, from Sarakhs down the valley, as recounted by Mr. Simpson, the special artist to the *Illustrated London News*, published by that paper, in its issue of the 21st March of the current year:

"The march from Pul-i-Khátun to Kojeh Saham-ed-din, and thence to Goolar, on our way to Kuhsan, was a very interesting one. The interest of it lies in its strategic features in relation to a force moving from Sarakhs on the line of the Heri-rúd towards Herát. From Sarakhs to Pul-i-Khátun the ground is open; on the left or Persian side it may be called a plain the whole way; but on the right bank a gentle rise begins at Kazil Koi, about eight miles south of Sarakhs. This rise assumes the character of a plateau or of undulating downs, all the way south to Pul-i-Khátun. Nowhere in that space is there any strong position of defence. At Pul-i-Khátun the whole character of the ground changes, the bed of the river becomes rocky, and perhaps about a quarter of a mile distant a gorge presents itself. Here the strata stand nearly perpendicular, and the road leaves the river to pass over the spurs of the higher hills on the south. This gorge, with one or two small heights, and the spurs just mentioned, could be easily made very formidable, if not impregnable; even as they are, a very small force could stop a very large one. Such is the position at Pul-i-Khátun itself; and it forms the key of the whole strategic problem. It is the Elburz Range which bends eastward, or south-eastward, to be more correct, at one of its ridges, the ridge dips down to the Heri-rúd, disappears, and crops up again on the east side of the bridge, from which it slowly rises towards the Zulfagar Pass. It is a common feature of the hills in this region to be steep and rocky, almost precipitous, on the south and south-west; while on the north the slope is easy. The ridge extending south-east from Pul-i-Khátun is of this character. For a few miles it is no great height, and there are one or two places where it might be passed by troops. The best place would be what is known as the Germab Pass, about nine miles from Pul-i-Khátun; this line takes the 'chord' of the curve which the river makes westward to Pul-i-Khátun. When the river is low, this pass is taken by travellers from its being the shortest line to Sarakhs. A force coming south could turn the position at Pul-i-Khátun by this pass, but if the defending force was large enough to extend along the whole ground to the Germáb Pass, it would have a strong position. The Germáb Pass, it will be understood, must form part of the whole position to be included as belonging to Pul-i-Khátun. South-east of the Germáb Pass, the ridge becomes so elevated and steep in parts that no force would try to surmount them. The next pass is that known as the Zulfagar; its southern entrance must be about thirty miles from Pul-i-Khátun, and the distance from leaving the river to the point where it is again touched by anyone coming through must be still greater; and I understand that no water is found in the pass itself. This will indicate one difficulty in marching troops by this line, on account of the want of water; and if there were a force defending the south end of the pass, the difficulty might be increased. The Zulfagar Pass is a very striking one, from the parallel ridges of level strata in the hills on each side, which rise to a great height.

"Kojeh Saham-ed-din is a saint's tomb, but our camp was at a spring of water about a mile from it. Our next march, to Goolar, was a very short one, being only eight miles. The deserted character of this part, since leaving Pul-i-Khátun, is even greater than anything we have yet passed. The ground has been cultivated at some former date; and we have seen spots on which towns have stood: now there is not an inhabited house all the way to Kuhsan. At Goolar we were in a piece of open country, with plains and heights, but of a small elevation, in comparison with the hills around.

"Our march from Goolar was at first for about seven or eight miles south, still on the west side of the Heri-rúd, which we had not seen since the march from Pul-i-Khátun —on that march we crossed it and re-crossed it again. Right across our line on leaving Goolar was the Kuh-i-Jam range; and our line south, over the lower ground, brought us to this range, which we began to ascend in a valley. On our left were four marked hills known as the Chakar Dowli— 'Chakar' meaning four. Between two of these the Heri-rúd passes out from the Kuh-i-Jam into the open country between that and the high ranges at Zulfagar. The gorges of the river where it passes the Kuh-i-Jam are impassable for travellers; hence the necessity for going over the hills. Our route lay up the valley in a south-westerly direction.

Troops could march by this road, but nothing on wheels could pass. We stopped for the night at an open bit of ground, where there was a stream of good water, with trees. On the top of a hill are some bits of the walls of a fort, called Stoi, but the Persians call it Istoi, and this gives the name to the Pass. We were said to be about 4,000 feet above the sea at this place, and it was very cold. There were clouds and a few drops of rain or sleet."

The party had four days' marches yet to perform to reach Kuhsan.

The distance from Herát to Sarakhs by this road is only two hundred and two miles. If the British Government and the British people are insane enough to allow Russia to shorten that distance by sixty miles—and that is the distance between Sarakhs and the Zulfagar pass—to occupy a place which is valuable only for its position, for it does not even possess a hut—we ought not to be surprised if we are soon called upon to yield Herát likewise!

I turn now to Panjdeh—or group of five villages—a long way within the Afghán frontier proper. A glance at the following itinerary between Herát and Merv along the valley of the Murgháb, on which Panjdeh lies on the direct line, will show more clearly than any special description the enormous importance of the position. I quote mainly from Captain Abbott's journal.

From Herát, due north, to Parwána, is eleven miles. The road lies between close hills, of no considerable height, and ascends the entire way. Around this village are hills and plateaux producing wormwood, which is browsed by the wild antelope. There are many wells and a little cultivation.

From Parwána the road leads across the mountain ridge of Kaitú, north-eastward by north to Khúshk, a two days' journey. Captain James Abbott, who made it in the year 1840, turned the difficult passes of the highest ridge and slept in a hollow where was a little water. From this he proceeded the next day "by a very distressing cross-country path, over steep hills covered with grass, to the rivulet Khúshk, whence we ascended to the capital of that name. The valley here is picturesque and interesting." The place, styled somewhat magniloquently as "the capital," is a small fort round which are mud houses and mud kibitkas or cabins. The valley of Khúshk is the dwelling-place of the Jamshidis, a tribe of Turkish origin, distinguished for their loyalty and their gallantry. The present condition of the place and the people is thus described by the *Times* correspondent in Bálá Murgháb, from whom I have already quoted :—

"On December 2nd we entered by narrow defiles the valley in which the Jamshidi or Jemshid settlement of Khúshk is situated. It is about fourteen miles long and of an average width of three-fourths of a mile; the hills are of low, rounded clay, bare of trees, their sides dotted with villages of domed mud cabins. The irrigation from the river is profuse, and there is much cultivation on the top and sides of the hills, where rain crops are grown. The grain raised is only sufficient for the wants of the people, and except in opium there is no export trade. Every Jamshidi family has its own home-bred horses, small wiry animals fit for any amount of work. The Jamshidis themselves are a quiet, tractable people, extremely friendly and well disposed to us. They were the first nomad tribe we saw at home, for though they have their mud cabins they only live in them during the winter, and at other seasons they prefer their kibitkas, which they are always prepared to take up and walk. Perhaps I ought to explain what a kibitka—the home of the nomad, and a very comfortable home, too—is like. Kibitka is the Russian and Ev the Turkoman name. It is a dome-shaped framework of lattice-work covered with layers of felt, the number of layers being in proportion to the severity of the weather. The walls for about 6ft. of their height are vertical and then the dome rises, its highest point being from 12ft. to 15ft. A felt cap fits on a hole in the centre of the roof which lets in the light—for the kibitka has no windows—when it is fine, and lets out the smoke when you light a fire on the ground underneath. The floor is generally spread with carpets of choice pattern, rich colours, and velvet softness, worked by the fair (?) fingers of the daughters of the kibitka; on the walls, too, hang camel bags, about 6ft. by 4ft., of the same rich carpet work. The great advantage of a kibitka is that in a few hours you can strike, pack up and load it on a camel and be off. Let Paterfamilias imagine the convenience of being able to put his comfortable house in the train and take it off to the seaside, and then he will understand that nomad life has its advantages. However, if on reading this description he wishes to send for a kibitka from Turkistan, he must not order a kibitka of such and such a size, but a kibitka which is a load for one, two, or more camels, as the case may be."

After dwelling upon the past recent history of this interesting tribe, and stating that, in the struggle between Ayúb Khán and Abdul Rahman the Jamshidis, having transferred their allegiance to the latter, had quitted Khúshk to take refuge in a less accessible valley, and had only returned when the cause of Ayúb Khán was irretrievably ruined, the writer thus continues:—

"However, the present Amir has moved 1,000 families back to Bálá Murgháb, an important strategic position which he wisely desired to colonize. Indeed, it was time that something of the sort were done, for, owing to over-population and over-irrigation the Khúshk valley had become very unhealthy, and the people were dying off fast from a sort of enteric fever which has been rife there the last few years. Aminulla Khán is the Governor of Bálá Murgháb and Panjdeh. There are still about 4,000 families in Khúshk—every four families are supposed to furnish one horseman in ordinary times—and I was much struck by the painful contrast between their physique and that of Jamshidis living elsewhere. The Jamshidis claim to be descended from a Kaianian Chief, who obtained from Sháh Abbas the command of a military colony composed of horsemen belonging to different tribes of Herát, and to this colony he gave the name Jamshidi, from Jamshid, the apocryphal progenitor of the Paishdadian and therefore Kaianian family. Sháh Abbas gave a district in Badghis to the Colony, and round the Persian stem thus planted there gradually clustered all the waifs and strays of Herát, till the Jamshidis mustered some 60,000 families. During Nádir Sháh's reign, however, they were reduced to 12,000, and they now number only about 6,000 families—namely, 4,000 in Khúshk, 1,000 in Bálá Murgháb, and 1,000 in Kurukh at the foot of the Kaitú mountains, four miles from Herát. The Jamshidis resemble the Turkomans in dress and manners, but they are apparently a quiet, peaceable people. An English officer might safely live among them without any guard, and if they have only respite from raids and war they will doubtless spread over and multiply in the more healthy but deserted lands of Badghis. They are hardy, clever horsemen, and every household breeds its own horses. When we were in Khúshk the weekly fair was held; it was attended by many Turkomans from Panjdeh and by some Firuzkuhis, but by very few Hazarehs, with whom the Jamshidis are not on very friendly terms. The Turkomans brought salt, rice, soap, carpets, horses, sheep, and found for sale in the bazaar ploughshares (of cast iron) and hatchets from Maimené;

Russian and French loaf sugar, Austrian matches, also Bryant and May's, Meshed and Bokhára silk and cotton goods. The greater part of the latter was Russian, not English—let Manchester draw its own conclusion."

From this valley the traveller bent on reaching Merv can either follow the rivulet of Khúshk by Khushak Sian, Chahill Docktar, Kala Tapa, Chaman-i-Baid, Kila-i-Maur, Pal-i-Kishti to Panjdeh; or he can proceed by the more direct road to Kála-i-Nau, thence to Pul-i-Taban on the Murgháb, and follow that river also to Panjdeh. Captain Abbott followed the first route, which he thus describes:—"We passed down the valley of the Khúshk rivulet averaging about half a mile in width, and bounded on either side by sloping, grassy downs, sprinkled with flocks of sheep and goats. Under the low, sunny cliffs and hills the Jamshidis had pitched their black tents in considerable numbers; and in the fields of the valley hundreds of mares and colts were grazing. The scene was extremely pleasing. The valley is highly susceptible of culture, and has once been well tilled." Captain Abbot encamped that evening at a point on the river between Púshat Siah and Kála Tapa. The next day he marched along a similar country to the latter place; beyond that, the day following, to within two miles of Chaman-i-Baid. Beyond Kála Tapa he met large flocks of sheep. "The shepherds," he writes "come even from Merv to this pleasant valley bringing water and all other necessaries on asses." The day after, as he marched to Kala-i-Maur, scenes almost similar met his gaze. "Large flocks of white sheep still sprinkled the hills on either side, but those hills were growing more arid and sandy as we advanced." Again, "We met not less than six or seven caravans of grain from Merv."

A few miles beyond Kala-i-Maur is Púl-i-Kishti* a spot

* Marked in Colonel Stewart's map simply by the word "Bridge."

which Russia has actually seized. It is only eight miles from Panjdeh. Here Abbott halted, and of it he wrote as follows: "Here the valley is about three-quarters of a mile in breadth. On the east bank are sloping sand hills, about 600 feet higher than the valley. On the west is the desert, a high sandy plain over-run with low bushes and camel thorn and extending to the mountain barrier of Persia." At Panjdeh to which he then proceeded, Abbott received the hospitality of the Turkomans who were then its occupants. He speaks of the desert as having been once populous and cultivated.

Not less interesting to us at the present moment is the alternative route by Kála-Nau and Moghor, to Pul-i-Taban on the Murgháb, and thence by way of Bála Murgháb and Maruchak to Panjdeh. Fortunately we are able, owing to the excellent correspondents of the London papers to see the country as it is at the present moment.

Kála-Nau is a valley which constitutes, so to speak, the capital of the Herát Hazárehs. It bears a strong resemblance to the Kúshk valley already described, except that it is smaller, more healthy, and more fertile. "The people," writes the *Times* correspondent, "are a branch of the Shiah Hazárehs of Hazáreh Jat, between Herát and Kábul, but, having become Sunis they have now no connexion with them." They are a very fine set of men, with pleasant frank faces, and with little trace of their Mongol origin. The influence of the present Amir over them is all-paramount:—"Every year," to quote from the same interesting source, "an increasing number of the Hazárehs still remaining in Persia join their brethren in the Kála-i-Nau valley, where there is plenty of room for them and many others The Hazárehs were at one time very troublesome to their neighbours, but they are now well in hand, and to quote the words of a native writer, 'Before

Abdurrahman Khán became Amir the Hazáreh Chief could murder his political opponents, but now he cannot.' I must say that I would not like to be in Mahomed Khan's way, had he a chance of removing me. He is a shrewd, self-contained, determined little man, with a quick eye, which is always intensely fixed on his own interests. The Hazárehs are very prosperous, not to say rich; their land is exceedingly fertile,—they have not much more to do than to sprinkle seed on the hill tops and wait for the friendly rain; and then, as they say, reap a hundredfold. Their chief wealth, however, is in cattle; of sheep they have enormous flocks. The Hazárehs of Kála-Nau afford another proof that the Amir's authority is absolute and unquestioned."

I don't think I can do better than allow the writer to continue the journey to Bálá Murgháb and to give his account of that place in his own graphic style:

"From Kála-i-Nau we might have taken the same road as Grodekoff and Vambéry, who travelled from Bála Murgháb by Talkguzar and the Darband pass, but it was not adapted to camel carriage, and accordingly we turned the mountains by following a stream which ran in a north-westerly direction through a succession of uncultivated valleys of great fertility, but at present only used by the nomad Ghilzais and Turkomans as grazing ground for their flocks. It was a long time since we had been in contact with Afgháns, and the discourteous manner—I daresay they could not help it—of these Ghilzais contrasted very unfavourably with the genial friendly attitude of the Char Aimaks and Hazárehs. About 30 miles from Ab-i-Kamri, the stream we were following was turned in a northerly direction to the Khúshk river by a high hill which stood in our direct path, while we wheeled to the south-west into the Torshek valley. Five miles brought us to our camping-ground by the side of a stream of very indifferent water. Close at hand too, was a hot sulpher spring, which in ancient days was apparently conducted into a huge bath, canopied by a brick dome said to have been erected by Sháh Rokh. On the 12th of December we reached Bála Murgháb, and as we neared the place from the south-east, the guns of the fort fired a salute of seventeen guns in honour Sir Peter Lumsden, who simultaneously entered the valley from the opposite side. The river was about 60 yards broad at the ford by which we crossed it, and not less than 3 feet deep. The current was very rapid, and though the ford had been skilfully staked, the laden camels had considerable difficulty in crossing it, and some would assuredly have been lost had it not been for the ready help given by the Jamshidi horsemen, who when a camel slipped or drifted down the current, swarmed round him like flies, whipped off his load and dragged him into safety.

"We are greatly pleased by our winter quarters, and everybody is well and in good spirits. Our camp is surrounded on three sides by the river in a valley about seven miles long and one or two miles broad, which runs from south-west to north-east, and is enclosed between two ranges of rounded clay hills. At the southern extremity there is a deeply indented gorge in the grand mountains of the Tirbund-i-Turkistán (which runs west to east) through which the Murgháb tears its way. At the northern end of the valley the hills gradually contract into a narrow defile for a few miles, when they again open out into the valley of Karaolkhana. Twice again do the hills thus contract and expand into the valleys of Meruchak and Panjdeh respectively. Panjdeh, I should add, is about forty-six miles from here. I have already explained that the Amir has colonized Bála Murgháb from among the Jamshidis, Firuzkuhis and Hazáras. This was a wise step, for Bála

Murgháb is a very important position strategically, situated as it is on the high road from the capital of Afghán Turkistán, and, perhaps, when the Russian flotilla of steamers is ready to navigate the Oxus, from Kerki to Herát. But it is not the sort of place that a timid English spinster lady would select as a residence, surrounded as it is, or to speak more accurately, as it was, by marauding Turkomans, unruly Aimaks, and the turbulant Uzbegs of Maimené. But now the Turkomans are tamed, the Char Aimaks peaceful, and Maimené has been subdued. Bála Murgháb is consequently a safe habitation. The colonies established there seem contented and prosperous. On the left or opposite bank to us there are the Firuzkuhi and Hazáreh colonies, and on this bank the Jamshidi colony. The happy family is awed into harmony by the fort with an Afghán garrison, and every day when we attempt to go out for a ride the flooded fields and numerous water-cuts remind us that the work of reclamation is being rapidly pushed on. I cannot say there is pretty scenery, though, no doubt, it is grand scenery, but there is the same want of trees which has characterized nearly every district we have marched through."

The route referred to by the correspondent as having been followed by Grodekoff and Vambéry, and which is the shortest and most direct route, is thus described by the latter:—"It is reckoned a four days journey for horses from Bála Murgháb to Herát. Camels require double the time, for the country is mountainous. . . . Two high mountainous peaks visible to the south of Bála Murgháb, were pointed out to us, and we were told that it would take us two days to reach them. They both bear the name Durbend (pass), and are far loftier, narrower, and easier of defence than the pass on the right bank of the Murgháb, leading to Maimené. In proportion as one advances nature assumes a wilder and more romantic appearance. The elevated masses of rock which form the first Derbend, are crowned with the ruins of an ancient fort, the subject of the most varying fables. Further on, at the second Derbend, on the bank of the Murgháb, there are the remains of an old castle. It was the summer residence of the renowned Sultan Husén Mirza, by whose order a stone bridge—Pul-i-Taban—was constructed, of which traces are still distinguishable. In the time of this, the most civilized sovereign of Central Asia, the whole of the neighbourhood was in a flourishing state, and many pleasure-houses are said to have existed along the course of the Murgháb.

"Beyond the second pass we quitted the Murgháb. The route turned to the right, in a westerly direction, towards a plateau closely adjoining a part of the desert peopled by the Salor. Here begins the lofty mountain, Telkhguzar, which it takes three hours to pass over.

"Towards midnight we halted at a place called Moghor, whence, next morning, we reached the ruins of the former town and fortress, Kála-Nau, now surrounded by a few tents of the Hazáreh."

Of Bálá Murgháb Vambery thus wrote; "this part of the valley of the Murgháb bears the name of Bála Murgháb;" (from the fortress of that name) "it extends from the frontiers of the lofty mountainous chain of the Hazárehs as far as Maruchak, where dwell the Salor Turkomans: it is said of old to have been a possession of the Jamshidis, and that they were for a time dispossessed and afterwards returned. To the south-west of the fortress the valley becomes so narrow that it merits rather the name of a defile. Through the midst the Murgháb rolls foaming away with the noise of thunder,—it is not until it has passed Panjdeh, where the river becomes deeper and more sedate that the valley spreads itself out and acquires a breadth of one or two miles."

Bálá Murgháb is 46 miles south-east of Panjdeh, Maruchak, also on the Murgháb, being about halfway between the two.

The following notes, by Captain Arthur F. Barrow, Aide-de-Camp on the staff of Sir Peter Lumsden, as to the military value of Pul-i-Khátun, were published in the *Illustrated London News* of the 14th March last:—

"From Sarakhs as far as Pul-i-Khátun, movement on either bank presents no difficulties. To Daulatábád, twelve miles south of Sarakhs, both banks are level; from that to Pul-i-Khátun, the right bank dominates, and all movements on the right bank are under cover, and fully concealed from observation from the left bank; while, on the other hand, no military movement whatever could possibly be carried on upon the left bank, within, at least, six miles of the river, without full cognizance of the right bank. The river itself, by reason of its depth and width, is nowhere a military obstacle. At Pul-i-Khátun, the road passes through a narrow gorge; it is a mere track with steep gradients, and thence, as far as Goolar, would present great difficulties to the advance of even a small flying column with the lightest guns. Without weeks of labour, it could not be relied upon as a main line of communication practicable for heavy artillery with its ammunition column, with the ambulance and the heavy-weeled transport and impedimenta of a large army. The river is, on the east side, shut out from Badghis by a steppe, which drops precipitously into it, the cliffs averaging from 150ft. to 200ft. in height. In this curtain there are two gaps, by which access to the river is obtained, called respectively the Germáb and Zulfagar Passes. From Goolar, our route lay to the west of the river, which passes, it is said, through an impracticable gorge; several other routes are, however, available—one by way of Zorabad, where water is found; and there is said to be very little natural obstacle to an advance beyond Goolar by those routes. Enough has been said here to show that the possession of Pul-i-Khátun, by any Power which anticipates advancing on Herát in the future, is a desideratum of considerable value; for access to the Pass would naturally result in the immediate construction of a good road, along a stream of excellent water. At the same time, it must not be overlooked that the impenetrable nature of the cliffs on the east bank of the river, render the use of this route, as a main line of advance, open to the very serious military objection that no lateral communication could exist with parallel lines of advance on that side; and that, in any combined movement, the force using this road might be met and defeated, at its exit, by a superior force of the enemy, while the other columns were being detained by inferior forces, occupying strong defensive positions. The occupation of Pul-i-Khátun by a weak Power, opposed to the advance of an army on Herát, and by one to which, owing to distance from its base, paucity of troops, or want of money, the conversion of Pul-i-Khátun into a defensive position is an impossibility, would at any rate result in the road remaining in its present condition; and would thereby deny its use to an enemy, at least for some considerable time after the declaration of hostilities."

The city of Kuhsan is thus described in the same paper, of the same date:—

"Kuhsan, sixty-eight miles from the city of Herát, on the frontier of the Persian Territory of Khorasán, stands on the Heri-rud where that river bends from a westerly to a northerly direction. The Heri-rud, a beautiful river fertilising and enriching the valleys of north-western

Afghánistán, rises in the highlands of Hazáreh, and flows from east to west between the broad mountain range which the Greeks named the Paropamisus, now called the Safed Koh or "White Mountain," and the Siah Koh, to the city of Herát, and thence to Ghorian, where it turns north-west to Kuhsan. This district, copiously irrigated by artificial canals, was once populous and wealthy; it is one of the most ancient seats of civilization. In the Middle Ages, during at least four centuries, Herát was one of the finest cities, and its province one of the most productive, in Central Asia. From Kuhsan to Sarakhs, by the road following the course of the Heri-rud, the distance is eighty-four miles. This is the road on which the Russians have recently advanced more than half way, seizing Pul-i-Khátun, nearly forty miles from Sarakhs, and recently the Zulfagar Pass, thirty miles higher up the river, where an opening through the wall of cliffs on the eastern bank gives access to the interior of Badghis, and through Ak Robat to the Khúshk valley and the Murgháb."

Panjdeh, and the road thence to Maruchak—the place above Bála Murgháb—are thus described by Mr. Simpson, special artist to the same paper. If the reader will recollect, the Russians claim to draw the new frontier line just above Maruchak (Little Merv):

"We stopped a day at Ak Tapa, and then moved on to Panjdeh. About six miles to the south nearly the whole distance is covered with Sarok villages, formed of kibitkas. The Sarok Turkomans have come south from the Merv district, and have become Afghán subjects. The Murgháb, as well as the Khúshk valley, was without inhabitants, and its fields were lying waste. Some years ago the Saroks arrived, and they have restored the place to life again. Some of their chiefs came along the Khúshk valley, and met Sir Peter Lumsden on the third march from Ak Tápa; crowds of the Sariks turned out to see our arrival, and the outskirts of the camp were generally fringed with them, eager to look at the Feringhis, and watch what they were doing. There was a good deal of trade going on in the purchase of carpets, and other articles, by our people. A considerable quantity of Indian rupees and Persian cráns was left among them, so we may suppose that they will retain a pleasant recollection of us. At Panjdeh we remained two days; one of these days was principally occupied by a visit from the Governor of Herát, who had followed us up; and Sir Peter Lumsden paid a visit to Yalintúsh Khán, the chief of the Jamshidis.

"There are the ruins, little more than mounds, of an old fort, and the evident remains of a town around it; these also are nothing more than mounds, on the west side of the river. A man called it "Kona Pendie," by which he meant old Panjdeh. If there is a new Panjdeh, we did not see it, unless it be the kibitka villages of the Sariks, and they extend for over twenty miles along both banks of the Murgháb. We were scarcely prepared for such a large sized river as we found here. It is as wide as Regent Street, of considerable depth, with a large volume of bluish-grey water flowing steadily past. When towns of importance, equal to those we have traced the remains of, come into existence again on its banks, "penny boats" will be shooting along from pier to pier. Fords are very few, and the one we crossed at Maruchak had at least four feet of water in its deepest part. I heard some one estimate the breath of the valley at Panjdeh as about four or five miles; whether this is exact or not, there is a large width of ground, which had been cultivated when the valley was prosperous and full of inhabitants. The mounds were the remains of large towns, and they are a sure evidence of the population that once exisited and found subsistence on the banks fertilized by the waters of the Murgháb.

"The march to Bund-i-Nadri was along the western side of the valley; about half way, the sandy hills on this side project considerably into the plain, narrowing it very much. Our road ascended the heights, but about a mile or so to the south we descended again, and found the valley nearly as wide as at Panjdeh. Our camp was pitched on a piece of level ground close to the hills. The Bund-i-Nadri was not far from us, but it turned out to be the old bund, which had been made on a bed of the river, which the water of the Murgháb had forsaken, and a new bund, or dam, higher up, was mentioned as having been made. The Bund-i-Nadri canal, a large watercourse for irrigation, flowed past close to us; it was filled with a beautiful clear stream. This is the canal whose water had been led, at some former period, across the Pul-i-Khisti.

"Our next march was also on the western side of the valley, along the base of the hills; and again we left the level soil, to pass through a hollow among them, which extended for some miles. On coming out again on the valley, we passed a Turkoman village, which I understood was the last of them towards the south. We struck across the valley to the river, where there are the piers only of a brick bridge standing. At this place there is a ford, which we crossed. Sir Peter Lumsden placed a number of Turkomans across the river, along the whole line of the ford, thus carrying out the military rule, which was very necessary, as the ford was far from being a straight line, and the current was strong. By this means all got over in perfect safety; even mild Hindús, on very small baggage-animals, who smoke and sleep instead of looking out where they are going, crossed scatheless. Our camp was formed close to the ford, and for the first time on the right bank of the Murgháb.

"Maruchak is on the same side; it is some distance from the river, and little over a mile from the ford. We were rather surprised at the extent of its walls, which would imply that the place had been inhabited at a later period than the other ruined towns we had seen. Our party found pheasants very plentiful at Maruchak, and there was some good shooting there. From Maruchak to Karaul Khaneh, which was the ground of our next march, has not yet been repeopled, and the whole space is at present in the condition of a vast game preserve. The birds flew up in great numbers, and when the sportsmen came in, covering the ground with long rows of dead pheasants, the only complaint heard referred to the defieiency of cartridges.

"After passing Maruchak, the hills change in their form; below that place they are undulating and rounded, but the curves have a very long radius. Above Maruchak they form small rounded knobs, with steep sides, all the way up to Bála Murgháb, to the south of which the geology entirely changes. The march from Maruchak to Karaoul Khaneh was on the right bank of the river. Towards the end of the march, we struck to the left, through a gorge formed by the steep sides of these mamelon hills, and came out again about a mile farther on. Karaoul Khaneh is the site of an old town; judging by the mounds, it had not been of great size. Here a valley comes in from the left, and, had the first idea of winter quarters beyond the Murgháb been carried out, we were to have moved in that direction. But a change had been made, and Bála Murgháb had been determined upon, so from Karaul Khaneh we marched, still on the right bank of the river, and came on here, arriving on Dec. 12."

The above extracts, made from many independent sources, will not fail, I believe, to convey to the reader a tolerable idea of the nature of the country of Herát, and of the immense importance to England of the continued possession by Afghánistán of the border line conceded to it in 1872—the straight line between Sarakhs and Khoja Saleh.

CHAPTER IX.

THE ARMIES ON BOTH SIDES.

As I write, this morning of the 25th of March, the air is full of rumours regarding a Russian advance on Herát. If they should prove true, it will devolve upon Peter Lumsden to play in 1885 the part which Eldred Pottinger played in 1838; to aid in the defence of the Pearl of Khorásán, until a British army can reach that city from the Pishin valley. In this view of the possibilities it is incumbent to glance, not only at the respective forces of the two nations, but at the distances which each must traverse before the battle ground can be reached.

On the subject of the armaments of Russia the *Daily News* appears to be singularly well-informed. In the issue of that paper of the 19th March appeared a statement of the numbers, composition, and distribution of the Russian forces in Central Asia, so important as to draw to it the attention of every politician and every soldier. Inquiries I made in other quarters likely to be well-informed, have satisfied me that the statement is in all essential points correct. It is as follows:—

The army of the Caucasus has not recently executed any movement indicative of dismemberment, and is still in that part of the country with the following exceptions:

1. Battalions of light infantry formed in 1880, and since that time quartered in the Trans-Caspian provinces:

No. 1, at Krassnovodsk.
No. 2, at Geok Tepé.
Nos. 3, 5, 6, at Askabad.
No. 4, at Tschikisjlar.

2. Cossacks.

Two regiments and two squadrons of Koubane Cossacks.

3. First Battalion of Railway Reserve.

ARMY OF TURKISTAN.

INFANTRY. FIRST BRIGADE.

1st Batt. 10th „ 12th „	Transferred to Taschkend, their habitual quarters, in the circumscription of Sir Daria.

SECOND BRIGADE.

3rd Batt. 6th „	Transferred from Samarkhand to Saravschan.
8th „	...Transferred from Kattibourgan to Saravschan
9th „ 11th „ 19th „	Transferred from Samarkhand to Saravschan

THIRD BRIGADE.

7th „ 4th „ 16th „ 18th „	Transferred from	Osch Namangan Andischan Kokand	to Ferghana.

FOURTH BRIGADE.

2nd „ 14th „ 15th „ 20th „	Transferred from Marghellane to Ferghana.

The 5th, 13th, and 17th Battalions do not form part of the above-named brigades. The 5th has been transferred from Petro Alexandrovski to the Amou Daria; the 13th from Marghellane to Ferghana. The 17th remains at Merv.

Four battalions of light infantry are in garrison at Taschkend.

Field Artillery.

1st	Battery	at Samárkhand	8 heavy pieces.
2nd	"	at Taschkend	8 nine-pounders.
3rd	"	at Andiskhan	8 light pieces.
4th	"	at Samarkhand	8 light pieces.
5th	"	at Taschkend	8 four-pounders.
6th	"	at Petro Alexandrovski	8 mountain guns, 3-pounders.
7th	"	at Samarkhand	8 mountain guns, $2\frac{1}{2}$.

Besides these, there is a battery mounted with six mountain guns (three pounders) in garrison at Marghellane.

Fortress Artillery.

3 Companies at Perovski, Taschkend, and Samarkhand.

Engineers.

Half a Battalion of Sappers } at Taschkend.
1 Detachment of Artisans }

Irregular Troops.

Regiments of Orenburgh Cossacks.

No. 4. Squadrons 1, 2, and 4, at Alexandrovski; 3, at Koungrad.

No. 5. Squadrons 1, 2, and 3, at Taschkend; 4, in Fort No. 1.

No. 6. Squadrons 1, 2, 3, and 4, at Marghellane.

One battery of Mounted Cossacks is at Taschkend.

Regiments of Oural Cossacks.

No. 2. Squadrons 1, 2, 3, and 4, at Samarkhand.

Troops from the Circumscription of Omsk.

Infantry.—Brigade of the Line of Western Siberia.

3rd Batt., transferred from	Djarkent	To Sémérétschinsk.
5th „ „	Kaurakol	
6th „ „	Kopal	
7th „ „	Verni	
8th „ „	Verni	
1st „ „	Omsk to Akmollinsk.	
2nd „ „	Garrison to Sémipalatinsk.	
4th „ „	Fort Saisanski to Sémipalatinsk.	

At Tobolsk, Tomsk, Omsk, and Sémipalatinsk there are also four battalions of reserve with the cadres for five companies each.

Besides these there are at Omsk another separate detachment and a military prison company. In several other towns and forts of Western Siberia there are altogether 44 separate detachments.

Field Artillery.

1st Battery at	Verni ...	8 light pieces.
2nd „	Djarkend	8 light pieces.
3rd „	Kaurakol	8 mountain guns (3-pounders).
4th „	Saisanski	8 pieces of small calibre and 2 mountain guns (3-pounders).

Fortress Artillery.

One company at Verni.

Engineers.

One company of Sappers at Omsk.

Irregular Troops.

Regiments of Siberian Cossacks.

No. 1. Squadron 2 at Ochonitchi, 3 at Kuldja, 5 at Koldschat, 1, 4, and 6 in Fort No. 4.

No. 2. Squadrons 2, 3, and 6 at Lepsinsk, 1 at Bachti, 4 near the river Chorgos, 5 at Djarkent.

No. 3. Squadrons 1 and 3 at Saisanski, 2 and 5 at Koton-Karagai, 4 at Kokpekti, 6 at Tschagan-Obinski.

Regiment of Semeretschinsk Cossacks.

Squadrons 2 and 4 at Verni, 1 at Djarkend, 3 at Narishu.

As to the composition and means of transport of their army, we are not without accurate information. Two days after the statement I have extracted from the *Daily News*, was published, there appeared in the *Times* a very interesting paper "On the Army of the Caucasus." Interesting as this paper is—and the reader is now again afforded the opportunity of re-perusing it—there are some points in it which seem to invite special remark.

"The operations of the Russian forces in Turkomania, of which the latest feature has been the seizure of places within the accepted boundary of Afghánistán, have attracted greater attention to the army of the Caucasus, which supplies the garrison of the Czar's recently-acquired possessions east of the Caspian. A great deal has been said about the formidable power of this portion of the Russian forces, and some military authorities have gone so far as to assume that half its strength would be available for a campaign against Herát, and that, without considering the armies of Turkistan and Orenburg at all, Russia could despatch from the Caspian, within a reasonable period of time, an army of nearly 100,000 men. The best way to ascertain how far these opinions may be deemed reasonable is to consider the actual composition and organization of the army which has its base and head-quarters at Tiflis.

"The army of the Caucasus has been roughly computed at 200,000 men, but in order to arrive at that total, all its details must be included, reserve, irregulars, and Cossacks. The regular army of the Caucasus numbers 70,000 men, but its reserve of another 50,000 would raise it to 120,000 strong. Besides this force of the line there are 30,000 Georgian and Imeritian irregulars of horse and foot. The Cossacks established in the settlements north of the Caucasian range, represent another section of the armed forces of the Tiflis Governorship, and they are expected to supply a quota of 50,000 men. These separate totals make up the grand result of 200,000 men, and this force may be properly compared and contrasted with the Anglo-Indian army of about the same nominal strength. It resembles that force in another respect which is too often obscured. A very large proportion of the army of the Caucasus is non-Russian. The Cossacks, Circassians, Georgians, and others form the majority of the troops whom Prince Dondoukoff-Korsakoff could array in time of war. The 70,000 men who are permanently engaged in garrison duty south of the Caucasus are distributed between Batoum, Tiflis, Kars, and other fortified places on the Turkish and Persian frontiers. They have also to furnish the troops employed in the Askabad district, and these number about 15,000 men, of whom 9,000 are in positions east of Bami. It is quite certain that any extra work thrown upon this portion of the Russian army would immediately necessitate the calling out of the reserves, who are really nothing more or less than military colonists who receive a grant of land and are allowed to marry after serving five years with the colours. The calling out of the reserves, and the increase of the Cossack regiments by the corps drawn from the steppe, would be the preliminaries to placing the army of the Caucasus on a war footing; but even then there would be plenty of work on its hands. It is within the range of possibility that the Russians could increase

General Komaroff's army to 50,000 men if they were left undisturbed in Armenia and on the Black Sea. But that task could only be executed at the cost of a great effort, and after the preparation of many months. In 1881, when Russia threw herself into the work of repairing the defeat of Geok Tepé and crushing the Turkomans, she succeeded in placing 25,000 troops on the eastern shores of the Caspian, but the preparations took nearly twelve months. Her permanent garrison in the Askabad province is now, as already stated, 15,000 men, and she has a railway from near Krasnovodsk to Bami. There is nothing incredible in the supposition that under these improved conditions she could in the course of the summer place 50,000 men on the northern borders of Persia.

"The composition of even the regular regiments of the army of the Caucasus is heterogeneous. Russians form a majority, but there are numerous Armenians, Poles, Jews, Tartars, and Russo-Germans. Circassians are also largely to be met with, particularly in the cavalry. But even the regular troops are subjected to a very light discipline, and if there is anything in our and German ideas as to military efficiency they can be little better than militia. A recent military traveller, who knows the Caucasus and Armenia well, and who does not conceal his identity under the pseudonym of "Wanderer," has given in his interesting "Notes on the Caucasus" the following description of the military routine of the regular army :—

"They have very few parades and absolutely no pipe-clay; a company or two is paraded daily during the summer months for rifle practice under the adjutant and musketry instructor, and the corps is assembled once a month for muster. The rest of the time the men do much as they choose, and usually either work at trades, selling the product of their industry at a sort of market which is held every Sunday in the bazaar of the town, or hire themselves out at so much per diem to private individuals as porters, labourers, &c."

"This sort of life is very different from the sustained military exercise to which our troops in India are accustomed, and, although the conclusion may be unsound, it will be generally considered that these soldiers would stand but a poor chance against our highly-trained European and Indian regiments. The Cossacks are excellent for all the purposes of irregular warfare, but they never have been trusted by any Russian General against a disciplined army in the open field, and of the 50,000 men whom Russia mght place east of the Caspian one-half would be Cossacks, as they are the most easy to mobilize and send on foreign service. The Cossack cavalry have attached to them a certain number of six-gun batteries of horse artillery, and these move about with them in the field. The regular artillery of the Caucasus numbers forty-three batteries of eight guns each, or 344 guns in all, and whereas the horse artillery consists of six-pounders the field artillery is composed of Krupp's nine-pounder steel breech-loading guns. The artillery is unquestionably the most efficient part of the army. The officers are well trained, and the men are specially picked for the service. The guns are admirably horsed and equipped. There are also a few batteries for mountain operations. With regard to the Georgian and other irregulars, it is declared that they are not inferior to the Russian regulars; but it is highly improbable that they would be employed outside the Caucasus. It is, of course, impossible to gauge with any degree of accuracy the comparative efficiency of two armies which are organized on two different systems and which have never met in war; but while admitting the merit of the Russian soldier, who is stated, without any excessive exaggeration, to be "capable of going anywhere on black bread and water," it does seem as if the superiority in military efficiency and military resources rested with the Anglo-Indian army rather than with that of the Caucasus.

"We have some practical experience of what the army of the Caucasus can do in actual warfare. In 1877, on the outbreak of the Turkish war, it could only place 50,000 men on the frontier, although preparations for war were begun in 1876. This force proved inadequate to cope with the Turks under Mukhtar Pasha, and the Russians were, as a matter of fact, repulsed all along the line in their first attempt to invade Armenia. At one period of the campaign, had the Turks pushed their advantage with greater vigour, or perhaps it would be more correct to say had they been better provided with the sinews of war, they could hardly have failed to achieve a decided success; but they allowed the opportunity to slip by, and when the winter of 1877 began the Russians had succeeded in arraying 100,000 men between Erivan and Poti. It must be remembered that this was only accomplished under compulsion and by a great effort. Yet the concentration of troops was on the nearest frontier of the Russian dominions, and the blow to be struck was against an enemy within 150 miles of Tiflis. Any campaign against Herát—for if war ensues Russia's objective will, of course, be the town on the Heri-rúd—would be of an entirely different character. Herát is 1,200 miles from Tiflis, and nearly 400 from Askabad; and although an army might be sustained once Herát is reached, most of the supplies for this force *en route* would have to be carried with it, after making the most liberal allowance for what might be drawn from Meshed and Northern Persia. The Russians, it is true, have 4,000 men on the Murgháb and nearly 5,000 between Askabad and Zulfagar, and those two corps, increased by a large Turkoman gathering from Merv, would undoubtedly suffice at this moment to overcome all opposition outside the walls of Herát. But in the event of Russia committing herself to the irrevocable step of an act of hostility against the Amir, it is clear that, although an initial success might be scored, it would be a matter of extreme difficulty, if not an utter impossibility, to raise the advanced army to anything like the large numbers that would be necessary in face of the joint opposition of the Afghan and Indian armies. We exclude from our calculations the effect that would be produced by an Anglo-Turkish alliance and the appearance of 20,000 English troops in Armenia. There is nothing chimerical in either proposition, and the army of the Caucasus is so far isolated that its communications with the rest of Russia are exceedingly difficult and subject to interruption. The army of the Caucasus will some day be more formidable than it is now, and when the railway system on the Western side of the Caspian as well as on the eastern is complete, it may be possible for Russia to throw the whole of her military resources into the effort to place 100,000 men on the Afghan borders. At present she could do nothing of the kind even with twelve months' preparation. The conviction that these facts are patent at Tiflis must strengthen the belief in a pacific settlement of the present difficulty, at the same time that they show that Russia has not the available power to maintain the aggressive position she has taken up on the rivers Murgháb and Heri-rúd, and that we have only to be firm in our declarations and to stand stanchly by the Ameer, to insure the speedy evacuation of those places south of Sarakhs and Yulatan which General Komaroff and Colonel Alikhanoff have within the last four months appropriated by force."

The sentences in this paper which appear to me to invite special attention, are those which speak of the difficulties which Russia would encounter in the event of her precipitating hostilities with the Amir. These difficulties may thus be classified:

1. The raising of the advanced army to anything like the large numbers that would be necessary in face of the joint opposition of the Afghán and Indian armies.
2. The danger that the Russian army might be isolated.
3. The difficulty of furnishing it with supplies.

I propose to consider these three points in detail.

Leaving for consideration further on the question of the entire force disposable in India, I would ask the reader to accept with me for a moment the statements which have reached us from that country by telegram, that there is at this moment a force of 30,000 men in the Pishin valley ready to advance by way of Kandahar as soon as they shall receive the order from Head Quarters. Accepting this statement, we must ask these two questions: what is the distance to be traversed; and how long will it take to traverse it.

The distance from the present advanced posts of the Anglo-Indian army to Kandahar is about 145 miles; from Kändahár to Herát is 369 miles. It is not easy marching, even when there is no enemy to be looked for. In the second Afghán war Stewart found the march even to Kandahar a very trying one. Unfortunately the intervening time has not been employed in the manner to which it might have been so usefully devoted—the making of a railway. Our armies will have to march as they did in 1839 and 1879-80. The difficulties, especially in the way of collecting carriage for such a force, will be as great now as they were then. Those who recollect how in 1881 Phayre's force was detained in inaction, at a critical moment, for the want of carriage, will appreciate the great extent of those difficulties.

The road to Kandahar is well known to our generals and our soldiers. I think that, having regard to the initial difficulties of starting, the best of these would admit that if he were to receive the order to advance to-morrow, he would think a fortnight not a day too long to enable him to reach Kandahar with 30,000 men. Sir John Keane, in 1839, marching as rapidly as he could march, took nineteen days to accomplish the distance from Quetta. Thence to Herát the road is less known, but it is certainly infinitely more difficult. I propose, in a few words, to describe it.

There are three important posts on the principal road between Kandahar and Herát—Girishk, Farrah, and Sabzwár. The distance by this road is 369 miles.

From Kandahar to Girishk the distance barely exceeds 75 miles.

The first march is to Kokáran—7 miles. The first 3 miles of road pass through the enclosed gardens and suburbs of the city. The road crosses the several canals drawn from the Argandáb for irrigating the Kandahar valley. At Kokáran water is abundant, the encamping-ground is well adapted for a large force, and forage can be supplied in sufficient quantities.

To Sanjári—5 miles. The bed of the Argandáb is crossed. The river, in the month of June, averages about two-and-a-quarter feet in depth, and the passage of it is easy. There is a ford about three-quarters of a mile lower down by which it would be advisible to cross heavy guns. Beyond the river one or two artificial watercourses have to be crossed. The road is stony in some places, but generally good. There is excellent encamping-ground at Sanjari; water is plentiful, and forage is sufficient.

To Hauz-i-Maddad Khán—14 miles. An excellent road across a broad, hard, level plain. A canal runs parallel to the road the whole of the march. The ground for encampment is good; water is plentiful near the camp; forage for camels is abundant; grass is scarce near the camp, but plentiful a few miles to the south of it. There are several villages in the neighbourhood; as well as flocks of sheep and goats.

Khúshk-i-Nakhúd—15¾ miles. A hard, level, gravel road without obstacle or difficulty. At Khúshk-i-Nakhúd water is plentiful, from two artificial water-courses; the encamping-ground is good; fodder for camels is plentiful; but grass, in the immediate vicinity of the camp, is scarce.

To Khak-i-Chapan—9¾ miles. The road generally good and level, though here and there the sand lies deep. The encamping-ground, though somewhat irregular, could easily be occupied by a large force. There is a sufficient, though not over-abundant, supply of water. Forage of all sorts is less plentiful. There are, however, villages and cultivation two or three miles south of the encamping-ground, as well as large flocks of sheep.

To Girishk—not quite 24 miles. The road to the left bank of the Helmund, about twenty-two miles and a half, is generally good and hard, the first part slightly undulating, with one or two sandy patches. There is a well about midway, but the water procurable from it is insufficient for more than a few travellers. On the left bank of the river is an excellent encamping-ground, with abundance of water and an ample supply of forage of all sorts. The Helmund is a difficult river to cross. In June its depth is about three feet nine inches; its width in the widest branch is seventy yards. The current runs at the rate of three miles an hour. There is a ferry which it is sometimes necessary to use. At Girishk the encamping-ground is sufficient, though here and there broken. Water and supplies of all sorts are abundant. I would add that, so far, the country is well known to our generals; it comprehends the districts which, as I have stated in a preceding page, would devolve upon us in the event of a permanent occupation of Kandahar by the British.

What Girishk once was may be gathered from the traditions of the time of Zaman Sháh. Even then people used to say that "the Helmund flowed through a garden." Now, though arable land abounds, there is but little cultivation. In fact, with the exception of the land immediately on the bank of the river, there is none. With peace and security for life the cultivation, however, would speedily revive!

The fort, though much dilapidated, commands a good view of the surrounding country. It is not, at present, capable of defence against artillery, but it might be made so with a comparatively small expenditure.

From Girishk to Farrah the distance, by the route adopted by Ferrier and Marsh, is 120 miles. There is a route by Shoráb and Hasan Gilan, shorter by 20 miles, but of this I have been unable to find any accurate record.

Girishk to Zirak—20 miles. The first six miles stony and undulating, the beds of several torrents crossing the line. The road then becomes level and easy till the fort of Saadat, 18 miles from Girishk, is reached. Saadat, once a rather strong, but, when Captain Marsh saw it in 1873, a deserted and ruined hill fort, has a plentiful supply of water. The road then becomes again undulating and continues so until close to Zirak. Zirak is a small village situated at the foot of the mountains on the right of the road to Herát and opposite Mahmudabad, described by Captain Marsh as a small village in a hollow watered by an artificial watercourse. At Zirak water is good and abundant, and forage for camels and horses is plentiful.

To Dúshakh—12½ miles. The road hard and level. Water at the village of Súr, about half-way. The encamping-ground at Dúshakh is good, and forage for camels and horses is abundant.

To Biabanak—three miles and a half. Road level, across a tolerably hard plain. There is an artificial canal at Biabanak providing plenty of water. Grass and fodder are abundant.

To Washir—24 miles. About four miles from Biabanak the road enters a range of hills with a gradual ascent to 900 feet, presenting no great difficulties. From this point to Washir the road winds among declivities, and follows the bed of watercourses, passing over much difficult ground. For the last 9 miles the road runs down a valley, with a gentle slope. It is hard and good till within 2 miles of Washir, when it becomes undulating and stoney. Many villages and gardens, watered by artificial canals are passed in this descent. Ferrier made the journey by halting during the heat of the day at Biabanak and then pushing on across the range, 20 miles, to Painak, but with no advantage over the route here laid down. At Washir supplies of all sorts, including water, are abundant.

To the Káshrúd river—14 miles. The road stoney and uneven, the last 4 miles being along a dry watercourse. The descent into the bed of the Káshrúd steep and bad. It is, however, practicable for artillery. The river supplies excellent water. Forage for camels abounds, but grass is less plentiful.

To Hájí Ibráhímí—14 miles. The fording of the Káshrúd is at certain seasons impossible, in consequence of the impetuosity of the torrent. In the hot season, however, the depth of the water does not exceed 18 inches. After crossing the river the road pursues a tortuous course among hills for about 3 miles; it then crosses a dreary steppe till it reaches Hájí Ibráhímí. Ferrier states that between Hájí Ibráhímí and Káshrúd there is not a drop water. Water and forage are both procurable at the former place.

Hájí Ibráhímí to Siah-áb—Ferrier calls this place Shiaguz—distance 10 miles. Siah-áb is the point whence a direct road, avoiding alike Farrah and Sabzwar, runs *viâ* Giraneh to Herát. It is an encamping-ground where water and forage are alike available.

Siah-áb to Kharmálik—22 miles. The first and last part of this stage leads the traveller through plains, fields, and marshes. The intermediate part is intersected by stony mountains, steeply scarped at the sides. "Kharmálik," writes Captain Marsh, "is situated in a small grassy hollow. A few date-palms and cattle, in the immediate neighbourhood of a few mean huts and wall-surrounded tower, are all it possesses." Water and forage are procurable here.

Kharmálik to Farrah—20 miles. The road leads across a desolate plain; then, over a low pass, enters a stony valley. Numerous ruins near the road indicate that the district was once well populated. The plain is totally devoid of drinking water.

"The appearance of Farrah a short way off," writes Captain Marsh, "is imposing. Its high embattled and bastioned walls, its broad, well-kept ditch, and fine large gate and drawbridge give it the air of wealth and ease. But what a delusion is this! On entering the city I was surprised to see its fallen state. The size of the interior is, perhaps, the third of Herát; but it does possess twenty huts, and those all in ruins. Where is the city of Farrah? Nowhere."

Farrah owes its destruction to the Persians and the Afghâns. In 1837 the Persians besieged and laid it waste because it belonged to Afghánistán. In 1852 the Barakzye Afgháns completed its destruction because it was dependent upon the Saduzye Afghán rulers of Herát. What Farrah was before the first of these events Conolly bore testimony in 1832. After speaking of it as a town possessing two thousand houses, he adds: "The land is fertile and much grain is cultivated, as the shepherds for many miles are supplied with it from hence. . . . The Furrah-rúd" (river of Furrah) "is in spring a wide and deep river, and there is always sufficient water for much cultivation." Ten years previously Mr. Fraser had described it as "a city as large as Nishapur, situated in a valley among hills with about twenty villages and many gardens." Again, I repeat, with peace and security for life and property its revival would be assured.

I have stated that from Siah-áb runs the direct road to Herát *viâ* Giráneh, avoiding Farrah and Sabzwar. It is worthy of consideration whether this route might not be ultimately made the main line of communication. It is shorter; and a force stationed at Giraneh would command alike Farrah and Sabzwar. Ferrier, after alluding to the strength of the fort as it was five-and-thirty years ago, thus writes regarding the position. "The position is important. It commands the passage of the river and the defiles in the mountains of the south. A small force quartered there might maintain its authority in the districts of Sabzwar, Farrah, Laush, Bakwa, Gulistan, Gour, and Sakkar, Giráneh being the central point round which converge these localities—information," he emphatically adds, "for the English and the Russians!" God grant that our countrymen may profit by the hint!

I may add that the road from Giráneh to Herát runs by Ab-i-Kúrmah and Sháh Jahán, and joins the Sabzwar road at Kash Jabran, a few miles above Sabzwar itself. The distances may be thus computed from Ferrier's journal. From Kash Jabrán to Sháh Jahán about nine hours caravan Journey, or about 20 miles; from Shah Jaran to Giráneh 56 miles. The country during the greater part of the way is described by Ferrier as well wooded and abounding in game, notwithstanding an almost entire deficiency of water.

I return now to the route by Farrah and Sabzwár. The distance between those two places is eighty miles. "There are," writes Captain Marsh, "no villages—a vast jumble of valleys and hills, with small plains, inhabited only by a nomadic people. Each place has its name, but if the traveller finds tents at the same place twice he is lucky." Captain Marsh accomplished the journey in three days, by Khúsh, Kilamúsha, and Darwázai. At each of these places he found water. Indeed, after the first 25 miles, the traveller follows, with a few deviations, the valley of the Rúd-i-Adrashkán. Regarding this river Ferrier observes that an army marching from Herát in the summer months should follow its course, as the commander would then be free from anxiety regarding the supply of water for his men and cattle. The hint should not be forgotten by an army which should march to Herát.

Sabzwár is eighty miles from Herát. It lies at the extremity of a large oblong plain, ten or twelve miles in circumference. The fort, prettily situated, is not formidable. The country around it is well cultivated, and abounds in flocks and herds. Water and supplies are abundant. A Híndú, who visited it in 1823, compared it, for fertility, with the best parts of Hindústán.

The road between Sabzwár and Herát needs no special description. It is good and level and passable for wheeled carriages of all descriptions. Supplies of all kinds are abundant.

The following are the stages—easily, if considered advisable, to be divided :—

Sabzwár to Kásh Jabrán—21 miles. Midway is a water reservoir, now in ruins. At Kásh Jabrán the direct road to Kandahar branches off, taking the route by Giráneh.

To Adrashkán—11 miles, about a mile on the Sabzwár side of the river of the same name.

To Sháh Beg or Bad — 23 miles. Five miles after crossing the Rud-i-Adrashkán the traveller reaches the Rud-i-Gaz, a rapid stream, fifteen or twenty yards broad, whose waters flow into the Adrashkán a little to the west of the village of that name. Six miles further the ruined caravansarai of Mír Allah is reached. It is surrounded by cultivation, and a fine stream of water runs under its walls. Six and a half miles further, again, the traveller passes a spring of sweet water on the left of the road. The dwarf reed, which provides sufficient fodder for horses, is here abundant; but the food of man has to be carried. Water is plentiful at Sháh Beg.

To Mír Dáúd—12 miles. The traveller descends from Sháh Beg. The descent is regular and gradual. The country is now uninhabited and uncultivated. Red and grey partridges abound. There is an artificial arrangement for the supply of water at Mír Dáúd, but under Afghán rule it has been but little cared for.

To Herát—18 miles. A good view of the city is obtainable from the last-named station. The traveller proceeds by a good road, 10 miles, to Rozeh Bágh, a royal garden—in olden days planted with Scotch firs of great size and beauty. Little more than 4 miles further on, the Herirúd is reached. The breadth of the river at this point is about a hundred and fifty yards. Its bed is here hollowed out, and its waters run in fifteen separate channels, twelve feet wide and very deep, enclosed between two embankments formed of the earth taken out for the excavations. To the south of the river is a fine piece of pasture-land formerly thickly studded with gardens and villages.

I think that, considering the difficulties of the ground and the necessity for carrying all his supplies with him, our general would be well satisfied if he could accomplish this distance in four weeks.

Granting, then, for the sake of argument, that the commander of the British expeditionary force were to set forth to relieve Herát, threatened by the Russians, on the 10th April next, he could not hope to reach that place before the 22nd May. And be it remembered, he would march at a time of year when the heat is the most terrific, and the water is most scarce.

What are the chances of Herát being able to hold out against a Russian army for three months?

Herát, it may be said, has held out against a Persian army aided by Russians, for ten months. That which has been accomplished once may be accomplished again.

I shall show, on the evidence of the man most capable to give an opinion, on the evidence of Eldred Pottinger himself, that such a contention, however pleasant it may be, cannot be sustained.

In the first place Russians with their modern arms of improvement are infinitely superior to the Persian army of 1838–9, with its flints and its popguns: in the second, Eldred Pottinger declared that the siege of 1838–9 failed solely because the place was not scientifically attacked.

It may be taken for granted that the defences of Herát are certainly not better than they were in 1838–9. They have been occasionally battered since, but they have never been repaired. We may have, then, an absolute conviction that the account given by Kaye* of the state of the fortifications of Herát in 1838 is not underpainted in its application to the present day.

"The city of Herát, it has been said, stood within solid earthen walls, surrounded by a wet ditch. The four sides were of nearly equal length, a little less than a mile in extent, facing towards the four points of the compass. The most elevated quarter of the city was the north-east, from which it gradually sloped down to the south-west corner, where it attained its lowest descent. The real defences of the place were two covered ways, or *fausse-braies*, on the exterior slope of the embankments, one within and the other without the ditch. The lower one was on the level of the surrounding country, its parapet partly covered by a mound of earth on the counterscarp, the accumulation of rubbish from the cleansings of the ditch. On the northern side, surrounded by a wet ditch, the citadel, once known as the Kilah-i-Aktyar-Aldin, but now as the Ark, overlooked the city. Built entirely of good brick masonry, with lofty ramparts and numerous towers, it was a place of considerable strength; but now its defences, long neglected, were in a wretched state of repair. *Indeed, when, in 1837, tidings of the advance of the Persian army reached Herát, the whole extent of the fortifications was crumbling into decay.*"

The italics are mine.

Such was, such is, Herát. Yet, being so, it successfully resisted a Persian army, aided by Russian officers, for ten

* "History of the War in Afghanistan." By Sir J. W. Kaye.

months. Upon that subject let us hear the opinion of the one Englishman within its walls, of the man of whom Kaye wrote: "The indomitable courage of Eldred Pottinger saved the beleaguered city."

"It is my firm belief," wrote that gallant Englishman in his journal, "that Mahomed Sháh" (the Sháh of Persia) "might have carried the city by assault the very first day that he reached Herát, and that even when the garrison gained confidence, and were flushed with the success of their sorties, he might have, by a proper use of the means at his disposal, taken the place in twenty-four hours."

That opinion, the opinion of a competent artillery officer, who successfully defended the crumbling ramparts, appears to me to be decisive of the question. It is clear that under ordinary circumstances Herát could not, if attacked now, resist a Russian force till the end of May. The only chance of her being able to do so would be the presence behind her ramparts of Lumsden and his companions. Lumsden is an experienced officer, and he has a very gallant following; but it seems to me, that if the Russians are provided with guns of the modern type, even the skill and courage of Lumsden and his companions could effect little, if it be true, as has been asserted, that the city can be commanded by a hill in its vicinity.

The reply, then, the reluctant reply, to the first query that Herát, if attacked now, could not hold out till the end of May, disposes, it seems to me, of the three questions raised by the *Times*. For, if the existing Russian force in the Transcaspian regions can take Herát before an English force could arrive before that city, and if, whilst the English force was advancing Russian reinforcements were likewise being pushed forward, it seems clear that the Power which has possession of the *point d'appui* must occupy the position of vantage. For whilst the English have to traverse 514 miles, over a barren country, all hard-marching, carrying their supplies, the Russians have to march along an easy road from Kizil Arvat, only 523 miles to Herát, drawing their supplies all the way, from the northern frontier of Persia. That northern part of Persia is, by the testimony of Napier and other eye-witnesses, already a Russian province, possessing agents in every village. The march, then, of the Russian reinforcements from Kizil Arvat to Herát, though nine miles longer, is a far easier march to accomplish than the march of the British force from the Pishin Valley to the same place. Under ordinary circumstances, then, the Russian advance force, far from being isolated, will be supported by a main body as strong as the advancing English army, before that army could reach Herát!

Nor is the argument regarding supplies more tenable. The base of Russia for supplies will be the northern frontier of Persia, between two and three hundred miles from Herát; the English base for the same purpose would be the country beyond the Indus, six hundred miles distant.

In connection with this subject, and as showing how much better prepared Russia is for her great spring than the outer world has any idea of, I annex here a letter written by Sir Edward Hamley in reply to one of the arguments used by the *Times*, upon which I have commented :—

"Seeing how inexpedient it is," wrote General Hamley on the 22nd March, "to underrate an enemy, perhaps you will allow me a few words of comment on your contributor's account of the Army of the Caucasus last Friday; by which I shall also hope to justify my view of the necessity of concentrating our resources on a war with Russia, if such is to be. Accepting your contributor's description of that army, and his estimate of the number of men which it brought against the Turks in Armenia in 1877, still that forms no measure of the forces which Russia could now assemble on the Caspian. For in 1877 the vast home army of Russia was entirely occupied in operating against the Turks on the Danube. It is now disposable for the reinforcement of the Army of the Caucasus. Troops embarked at Odessa would reach Batoum in two days, the Caspian in three, and the present end of the Transcaspian Railway at Bami within the week. Nor would the severance of the communication across the Black Sea prevent the transit, for many railways cross Russia to debouch on the Volga, which forms a vast highway to the Caspian. Thus, the trial of strength would be not between the Army of the Caucasus and the Army of India, but between the forces which the two Empires could bring to bear in the theatre of war.

"Further, during the war of 1877, Persia, as a neutral, assembled an army of 40,000 men for the protection of her own soil. If that army were directed against us, in alliance with Russia, it would march by excellent roads within the Persian frontier to Meshed and the Heri Rud. If there is anything in the task that would thus be set us to authorize the belief that, besides dealing with it, we could also maintain a British force of the present strength in Egypt, I shall rejoice to hear of it, but I have failed to discover it."

The argument of this letter is unanswerable. It goes to confirm my conviction that unless an English force can reach Herát before Russia, take possession of that city, the entire province, which has been for ages the bulwark of India, will be for ever lost.

What, meanwhile, is our position in India? We can dispose, in that country, of a regular force, inclusive of the troops which have been lent to England for the Soudan, of 61,736 European, and 125,695 native troops, counting officers. The following table shows their component parts :—

NATIVE ARMY, INCLUDING OFFICERS.

Artillery	1,835
Cavalry	18,824
Infantry	101,926
Sappers and Miners	3,110
Total	125,695

BRITISH ARMY, INCLUDING OFFICERS.

	Bengal.	Madras.	Bombay.		Total.
Artillery	6,209	2,491	2,786	=	11,486
Cavalry	2,868	956	478	=	4,302
Engineers	201	43	48	=	292
Infantry	29,222	8,217	8,217	=	45,656
	38,500	11,707	11,529	=	61,736

This is the peace establishment, a total of 187,431, to guard India, and, we will hope, to maintain Herât. Of course it may be greatly increased. It is satisfactory to learn that Lord Dufferin has already issued orders that two hundred men shall be added to each regiment, and equally so that enlisting has again become popular in India. It is an additional satisfaction to feel that the destinies of India are in the hands of a man who possesses the absolute confidence of the English people.

The exact mode in which the army available for field service may be employed must depend on circumstances. England knows that her generals on the spot, if left unfettered, will conquer even the impossible. But they may read, as every one may study, with advantage, the words uttered last May on the subject by our most accomplished strategist :—

" I will suppose Russia," said Sir Edward Hamley, " to have made her next step—a step which need surprise nobody; many Indians look on it as already virtually accomplished—and occupied Herát. We know when she will do this—in a moment of perplexity to England. As to the how, perhaps by first occupying it with a Persian garrison (not to alarm us too much), and afterwards, by some subsequently announced Treaty, replacing that garrison with Russian troops. This may easily be done before we are aware, especially if we follow the plan of respecting Russian susceptibilities so far as not even to keep ourselves informed of what she may be doing. And it was a feature of Skobeleff's plan of invasion, now become absolutely feasible, 'to organize masses of Asiatic cavalry, and hurling them on India as our vanguard, under the banner of blood and rapine, thus bring back the times of Tamerlane.' We may therefore wake up to find this programme in execution, with Russian troops to any extent massed along the line of the Transcaspian railway, ready to support those in front. Now, on our side, we have of late increased the force at Quetta, and planned a system of local defence for Beloochistán; but our comparatively insignificant field force is 220 miles from the Helmund. That is one case. The other is that we had a strong British Governor in Kandahar, and a strong British force on the Helmund and on the road to Kábul—the railway completed to Kandahar—in case of a movement from Turkistan against Kábul, a force on our side on its way to occupy that city, if not already there, and new recruiting grounds open to us amid warlike populations. Surely there can be no question as to which of these two sets of circumstances would give us most influence in Afghánistán, most power to oppose Russia, and to maintain confidence in India. And we must remember that four years ago we could have done this and more than this. The whole country was going to pieces for want of strong rule. We were actually hunting for rulers. We set up one at Kábul, and another at Kandahar, who was soon afterwards removed, and the whole country placed under the present Amír. Before and since that event the unwavering theory of successive Governments of India has been that the Amír is to be kept from Russian influence, and to be maintained and supported in alliance with England. But when we ask what steps have been taken for carrying this theory into practice, I fear we shall not find much that is satisfactory. Perhaps the utmost we could in present circumstances promise ourselves, in meeting a Russian advance, would be that after heavy fighting and vast expenditure we should succeed in gaining those positions which are now open to our grasp, and our presence in which might obviate the risk of war.*

"I have said nothing about a British occupation of Herát. Yet that too was open to us four years ago, and not only open to us, but contemplated, in certain contingencies, by the Government of India. If I refrain from speaking of it it is because I fear at the outset to excite the opposition, and possible refusal to consider any forward movement, of those who are already hampered by the opinions they formerly expressed. I am aware, too, of the strong reasons that exist against straining our resources by embracing points so distant in our first operations. But I will confess that as an abstract military plan for the defence

* "And here I may mention that, since this paper was printed, I have seen evidence that most of the views here set forth are shared by an Indian Officer whose name would be at once admitted as of almost decisive influence in the question."

of India under present conditions, and supposing sufficient additional troops to be forthcoming, that which most strongly recommends itself to my mind is a strong British Government at Kandahar, wielding an army whose advanced troops should be at Kábul and Herát, based on Kurrachee, with railway communication at least thence to Kandahar. I believe it is considered that great part of such an army could be supplied from our present Indian forces. However, I will not enlarge on this plan, though I imagine it is what a strong Power, thinking more of security than expense, might be expected to adopt. But, assuming that we wish to keep our hold on this rampart of India, it is urgently necessary to take steps while the Russian preparations are still undeveloped. We must at once obtain such a settlement of its boundary as I have endeavoured to sketch. And military reports on the whole country, from this frontier to positions securing or commanding Herát, and thence to the Helmund, should be framed forthwith. Our ignorance of all this is, considering its importance, astonishing. While Russian officials have explored up to and beyond Herát, and elsewhere along the Afghán and Indian frontier, our own officers have been discouraged, indeed prohibited, from obtaining personal knowledge of those regions, so that the scanty information I have been able to give about them is from those who acquired it almost by stealth. An extreme care not to wound, by showing suspicion, the innocent candour of those guileless beings, Russian statesmen, appears to have been our ruling motive, and is probably dignified by the name of diplomacy. The frontier is most important to us, yet no one can say where the frontier is. In a few years we may be fighting on the Helmund, or the Heri-rúd, yet we know nothing of the military features of the region."

One word in conclusion as to the composition of the

Anglo-Indian army. Of the British troops I need say nothing; but with respect to the Indians I am glad to be able to express my absolute conviction that a Sikh regiment, led by British officers, is quite the equal of a Russian regiment; that a Gúrkha regiment, similarly led, is likewise, at least the equal of a Russian regiment; that the Gúrkahs of Nepál, led by British officers, are equally as able to meet the shock; that the Indian Irregular Cavalry can successfully dare the Cossack to any encounter. The material, then, of the force which may have to meet Russia on the frontier of India is all that can be desired. The only fault is that it is so small. I repeat, then, the advice which has recently been so strongly urged upon the Government by the one strategist who has never been at fault: I would urge them to abandon the position in the Soudan, where—to use the words of Louis XV. at the battle of Laffeldt in 1747—"England fights for all and pays for all," to the advantage of the "all," and to transport the army employed there to the spot in India where the dearest interests of our country are threatened. It would be necessary to stipulate, if this policy were carried out, that the General-in-Chief should be left behind. Lord Wolseley might replace the heroic Gordon in a new Khartoum. We have yet, in India, in Roberts, in Charles MacGregor, in Donald Stewart, in Macpherson, and in others also on the spot, men who have proved, on the hardest and most trying of fields, that "whilst no military qualification is wanting, the fount of honour is full and fresh within them." In England, too, in the able and cultivated commander who stormed Tel-el-Kebir, who has studied the question of the Indian frontier, in a way such as no man but Charles Macgregor has studied it—in Sir Edward Hamley—we possess a leader the compeer even of such men as these!

CHAPTER X.

RUSSIA'S ATTACK ON PANJDEH AND ITS MOTIVE.

No cause was ever advanced by exaggeration. The cause I am pleading in this chapter is the cause of the English people. Before I conclude it I shall show how their prosperity is bound up in the maintenance of our Indian empire; how the loss of that magnificent dependency would affect the position of every man, every woman, and every child in these islands from the highest to the lowest. Convinced as I am that the occupation by Russia of Herat, the outlying fortress which covers India, would be the prelude to an invasion of India, I shall indicate the purpose which has prompted the Russian general on the spot to make that sudden attack on the Afghans of Panjdeh which roused all England to indignation on the morning of Thursday, the 9th April. And, that I may not be accused of exaggeration I shall, in describing that attack, quote the words used in the House of Commons on Thursday evening by one who has lost no opportunity of declaring his faith in Russia: who, addressing his present constituents in 1879, declared that he had "no fear of the territorial extensions of Russia, no fear of them whatever;" that he thought "such fears old women's fears"—I shall quote the words used by the Prime Minister of England.

In a previous chapter I showed that when the British Commissioner, Sir Peter Lumsden, arrived, in accordance with an arrangement agreed to by the Government of the Czar, at Panjdeh, he was not met there by the Russian Commissioner, but that, shortly after his arrival, Russian troops seized the posts, important, because valuable for aggressive purposes, of Pul-i-Khátun, Zulfagar, and Pul-i-Kishti; that the British Government had addressed serious remonstrances to St. Petersburg on the subject; and that, after a very slight discussion it had been arranged between the two Governments that Russia should retain the positions her troops had occupied, pending the definition of the frontier by the Commissioners of the two nations. The arrangement was generally regarded as a very unsatisfactory arrangement for England, but it had been made by the British Government, and the British people, with a great deal of smouldering disgust, and with a strong conviction that they were being duped, were obliged to await the result.

The Ministers of Great Britain duly communicated this agreement to Sir Peter Lumsden. It may be presumed that the Ministers of Russia likewise duly communicated the agreement to their general on the spot—the general commanding at Pul-i-Kishti, General Komaroff; although that general informed Captain Yate that he had not received it. Whether he received it or not, is a matter between himself and his Government. It is clear that the Ministers of Russia are responsible to the Ministers of England for the due observance of the arrangement made between the two nations. From those Ministers must the British Government demand reparation.

On the morning of Thursday, the 9th April, the public were startled by an announcement made in the *Standard* newspaper that the agreement between the two countries had been violated, and violated by Russia; that Russian troops had made a premeditated attack upon the Afgháns. Second editions of the other morning papers confirmed the news which the *Standard* had been the first to announce.

That same evening the Prime Minister of Great Britain explained the matter in the House of Commons. After some introductory remarks, he said :—

In the first place there are two things admitted—namely, that an attack was made on the Afgháns by the Russians and that the Afgháns were defeated. On those two points there is no doubt —defeated, as we are informed, after a gallant fight. The Russian allegations are mainly these. I will not attempt to give them in strict form, but the House may depend upon the substance of my recital. The Russians attacked the Afgháns, as they state, after being provoked by acts of hostility so termed—the nature of which we are not distinctly informed of—on the part of the Afgháns. When the fighting was over the Russians retired. They retired, according to a phrase used in one document, to their previous positions, according to the other document, to the left bank of the Khushk. These two phrases may be exactly equivalent. I am not prepared to say they are not, but I mention them both because they are used in the two accounts which have reached us. It is next alleged that English officers directed the Afgháns without taking part in the actual engagement, and finally it is stated that the Russian commander sent an escort to protect the English officers after the Afgháns were defeated, but that the English officers had themselves left the ground when the escort arrived, so that there was no occasion for it to act. These are the principal allegations that have reached us as the allegations of the Russian Government.

The date of the engagement is the 30th of March, and perhaps I may say that the earliest intelligence of the most material of the facts I am about to recite only reached Lord Granville and myself this morning. Well, now I come to the allegations made by Sir Peter Lumsden and our own officers, to which I need scarcely say that, as a matter of course, we give credit, and which undoubtedly call for very grave attention. In the first place it is stated that no forward movement of any kind was made by the Afgháns before or since the 17th of March—the 17th of March being the date of the telegram I shall now recite. On the 29th of March we were informed—and when I say "we" I speak of Sir Peter Lumsden's telegram sent to us—we were informed that, notwithstanding the Russian assurances of the 17th of March—this is the substance of the telegram which the House will no doubt recognize, because it was the substance of the statement made by me in this House and sent to St. Petersburg and recognized there, and returned thence with a certain addition stated in this House at the time—on the 20th of March we were informed by Sir Peter Lumsden that, "notwithstanding the Russian assurances of the 17th of March that the Russian forces would not advance from the position they then occupied provided the Afgháns should not advance nor attack them, or unless some extraordinary circumstance should happen, such as a disturbance in Panjdeh, the Russians were drawn up in force almost within range of the Afghán position, though the Afgháns had neither attacked nor advanced, and Panjdeh was perfectly quiet;" that every endeavour was being made by the Russians—this is in the nature of a general statement—to induce the Afgháns to begin the fight; and that the Russian forces had attempted to forcibly pass through the Afghán pickets. The next point is that on the failure of those attempts Captain Yate met the chief of the Russian staff by appointment, and was informed that no such arrangement as that referred to in the telegram of the 17th March as to the non-advance of the Russians had been received. ("Oh.") This has been made the subject of proper communication. Next, that the chief of the staff, whose name I do not recollect, would not give an assurance to Captain Yate that the Afgháns would not be attacked without previous notice, and he claimed the right to turn out the Afghán posts whenever they might inconvenience the Russians, without reference to any third party. That, of course, must be taken in connection with the statement immediately preceding—that he had not received from St. Petersburg instructions corresponding with the telegram of the 17th March. Next we learnt that on the 29th of March Sir Peter Lumsden desired Captain Yate again to see the Russian commander and effect an amicable arrangement if possible. We learnt, on the 7th of April, that down to the 30th of March the Afgháns had made no forward movement before or since that telegram of the 17th of March. On the 7th of April we also learnt that Captain Yate had, on the 1st of April, sent a note from a point which he had reached with all the British officers and escort safely on the previous day at 8 P.M. on the way to Gulran. It stated that the Russians had attacked and defeated the Afgháns, and had occupied Panjdeh on the 30th. The Afgháns were said to have fought gallantly and to have lost heavily, two companies being killed to a man in their entrenchments. The survivors retreated along the Maruchak road. The British officers were neutral in the engagement. The House will not be surprised when I say, speaking with measured words in circumstances of great gravity, that to us, upon the statements I have recited, this attack bears the appearance of an unprovoked aggression. (Cheers.) We have asked for explanations from the Russian Government. There has not yet been time to receive such explanations. We shall endeavour to arrive at a just conclusion on the facts. But before receiving our communications yesterday, and when we had not the important communications of this morning, but something preliminary in the same direction, the British Ambassador at St. Petersburg reported to us last night at forty minutes past five in these words :—" The Minister for Foreign Affairs expresses his earnest hope and that of the Emperor that this unhappy incident may not prevent the continuance of the negotiations " (laughter) ; and he also reported a statement of M. de Giers that the Russians retired to their previous positions and did not occupy Panjdeh. I may say that I have laid these statements before the House as being the incomplete and partial statements which the very short time that has elapsed since the receipt of the news alone enables me to offer, and they are as much as our public duty will permit us to make ; and I think I may say that they comprise the whole of the material statements of fact which have reached us upon this important, and for the moment I may say very painful, matter.

Later on, during the same evening, the Prime Minister supplemented the above statement with another. He said :—

" I had intended, either on the motion to report progress or on the actual report of the resolutions with the Speaker in the chair, to mention that since I spoke at the commencement of the evening a telegram has been received from Sir Peter Lumsden, which conveys what I may call a qualification of one of the statements which he had made. The statement I made on the authority of Sir Peter Lumsden was, as will be remembered by the House, because I repeated it twice, that the Afghâns had not made any advance either before or after the arrival of the telegram of the 17th of March. But Sir Peter Lumsden states to us in a later telegram that when the Russians immediately threatened an attack on the Afghân position by advancing in force to Ak Tapa, the Afghâns threw out vedettes to their front and extended their pickets to Pul-i-Khisti, on the left bank of the Khushk, and gradually strengthened it until on the 30th, the bulk of their force had been transferred across the river. That is the qualification which he conveys. He goes on to say that, in his opinion, that does not properly constitute an advance, but was the occupation of a more advantageous position. But I presume he evidently considers that the question might be raised as to what did or did not constitute an advance, and he is desirous that the British Government should be placed in the possession of all the facts. I give the qualification to the House precisely as Sir Peter Lumsden has given it."

To this statement by Mr. Gladstone I may add the more recently received explanation of General Komaroff:—

"On the 25th March our detachment approach Dash Kepri. On our side of the river Khushk, close to the bridge, I found an intrenchment occupied by the Afgháns."

It is not necessary to continue. If Komaroff did not want a conflict why did he approach an intrenchment "occupied by the Afgháns"? The term, "our side of the river," proves that Komaroff had prejudged the question. The river runs through territory which has been tributary to Herát since 1863, and even earlier!

Now, what is this story, summarized in a few plain words? It is simply, that the Russians at Ak Tapa threatened to attack the Afgháns at Panjdeh; that, on seeing the Russians advance, the Afgháns, not caring either to run away or to remain in a defenceless position to have their throats cut, took up a new alignment; that the Russians then attacked defeated them, and took Panjdeh; that the Afgháns then retired to Maruchak. The Russians, by their action, gained perfect command of the route leading by the Khushk valley to Herát, the route traversed by Captain Abbot in 1840, and described in pages 136-40 of this book; and they now face Maruchak, about midway between Panjdeh and Bala Murgháb, covering another road to Herát, the road traversed by Vambéry and Grodekoff, described in pages 144-6.

Now Russia is a great Power, and Afghánistán is the subsidised ally of England. The Amír of Afghánistán is in fact paid by England to guard the outlying redoubt which covers the approaches to India. That outlying redoubt is the country known under the generic name of Herát. It comprises the city of that name, the valleys of the Heri-rúd, the Khushk, and the Murgháb, as far as Sarakhs on the one side and Robat Abdullah Khán on the other. This territory has been violated in a time of profound peace by a Power which, only fifteen months ago, was far removed from the extremest border claimed by the Afgháns, and which has since insidiously crept up to that border.

If such a thing had happened in Europe; if, for instance, France, in 1867-8, had suddenly pounced upon the Duchy of Luxemburg, which had been given to her by the King of Holland, would Germany have allowed it for a moment? The march of a single regiment across the border of that Duchy would have been accepted as a declaration of war. Why, the very claim to Luxemburg made by Napoleon III. very nearly brought about such a result! Is there, then, to be a law of nations in Europe, and no law of nations in Asia? Are we to be swift to repel on the one continent, and to turn our face to the smiter on the other? I ask this question because we are, at this moment, turning our face to the smiter on the banks of the Murgháb, and unless we suddenly recoil, and put down both feet, and, pointing to the frontier of 1872-3, say to the smiter, "thus far shalt thou come but no further," we run the greatest risk of losing India.

These are not empty words: they are words of truth and solemn warning. Any one who chooses to read between the lines can detect easily enough the reason for the action of General Komaroff. To those who cannot I will explain it.

First, let me recall to the recollection of the reader the general principle of the policy of Russia as described by the statesman of this century who knew her thoroughly, by the lamented Lord Palmerston. The words are quoted at pages 38–9 of this volume. Let the reader apply them to the action of General Komaroff and the excuses made by M. de Giers, as that action and those excuses have been stated by Mr. Gladstone. "The policy of the Russian Government," wrote Lord Palmerston, "has always been to push forward its encroachments as fast and as far as the apathy or want of firmness of other Governments would allow it to go." "In furtherance of this policy the Russian Government has always two strings to its bow—moderate language and disinterested professions at St. Petersburg and at London; active aggression by its agents on the scene of operations. If the aggressions succeed locally the St. Petersburg Government adopts them as a *fait accompli* which it did not intend, but cannot in honour recede from. If the local agents fail they are disavowed and recalled, and the language previously held is appealed to as a proof that the agents have overstepped their instructions." Is it possible to describe more exactly, with more absolute precision, the courses which Russia is now pursuing at London, at St. Petersburg, and on the Murgháb? She has adopted the aggressions made by Komaroff as *faits accomplis;* she has, if we may believe the St. Petersburg correspondent of the *Times* (11 April), *conferred decorations and rewards, by telegraph, upon those engaged;* while she has been assuring us at St. Petersburg that such aggressions were made in spite of her instructions. She adopted those aggressions because our Ministers had not the "pluck"—there is no other word for it, and it is a right good English word—to tell her that unless she retired there would be war!

For, let us consider, why is Russia making this spring just at this particular moment? *She wants the city of Herát.* To gain that city is the end and aim of all her movements. Herát is comparatively weak now; her fortifications are in disrepair; there is no English force within five hundred miles of it. If Russia can only get possession of Herát now, no power on earth will ever take it from her. The plains and the valleys follow the city. If she can only gain Herát now she gains a new base where she can rest and wait for the opportunity to pounce upon India.

Yes; that is the cause of these aggressions which in spite of their being disavowed are invariably accepted; this is the meaning of the smooth words which serve to gain more and more time for Komaroff and Alikhanoff! Whilst Russia is protesting in London, her generals are advancing down the Khushk, the Murgháb, and the Heri-rúd. Her secret purpose is to seize Herát before India is ready, before British troops can be sent to the scene of action from the Soudan—to seize it, to fortify it, and to use it as a menace to India!

What the effect upon India of the acquisition of Herát by Russia would be, I described in language to which I can add little, in a paper I wrote for the Patriotic Association in 1879. What, I asked then, will mean the occupation of Russia by Herát? I added:

It will mean simply this: that the gateway leading into our Indian Empire has been occupied by our enemy. It will mean that henceforth there will be no peace for the people of India, no security for trade, no money for improvements. The English in India will live under a continual threat—not at first of invasion, but of the intrigue which corrupts their native soldiers, which wins over their native allies, which makes every man doubtful of the morrow. In a word, they will live in a fortress which is being mined, and which they will know is being mined. . . . . India would resemble a tenanted mansion, the keys of the doors of which were held by robbers daily engaged in attempting to corrupt the servants on the basement. What would become of her revenues then? Industry, the cause of the wealth of nations, would be paralyzed, and a few years would witness a national bankruptcy.

In a word, the occupation of Herát by Russia would be a permanent menace to India.

Another attempt is now being made by Russia to hoodwink our ministers, and again have our ministers been hoodwinked. They have accepted the assurances from

St. Petersburg that no reply can be received from General Komaroff for seven or eight days. Now, on this point, I have received a communication from a gentleman well acquainted with the Trans-caspian regions, which he has permitted me to use. He writes: "The *Daily Telegraph* is right in stating that the Russian telegraph line extends to within 120 miles of the Russian posts near Panjdeh. As the Russian couriers are compelled to travel at the rate of ten miles an hour it is clear that it would require but twelve hours to receive despatches from St. Petersburg." The cause of this deceit is obvious: it is to gain time to carry out the nefarious design against Herát!

In a hostile criticism on the first edition of this book, the writer, a Blue-ribbonite, remarked that there was a large and growing number of Englishmen who were inclined to regard India as a dead weight on the people of these islands. It is scarcely necessary to reply to the ignorant folly displayed in such a remark, but as there are many who are not aware of the manner in which these islands benefit by the connection, I think a useful purpose will be served if I conclude this chapter with an extract from a lecture delivered on the subject in the theatre of the Society of Arts on the 4th March, 1881, by one of the most accomplished and instructed of men, Mr. J. M. Maclean. "It is hardly necessary," said Mr. Maclean in the body of his admirable address, "to insist upon the obvious material gains which accrue to England from the possession of an Eastern Empire. A simple enumeration of them will suffice. In the first place it is no slight advantage to us that the Government of India disburses in this country 16 millions sterling a year, out of the revenues collected from Indian taxpayers. The English nation, it is true, does not take this money from the people of India without giving them something in exchange for it." After stating the nature of the exchange Mr. Maclean thus continued :

"The indirect gains of private enterprise in India are also very considerable. British India ranks now with France, Germany, and the United States among our best customers. The United Kingdom supplies her with three-fifths of her whole import of merchandise. . . . . Nor do Englishmen make profits only on the import trade into India. The greater portion of the export trade is controlled by English houses, settled in Presidency towns ; and four-fifths of the shipping engaged in the following commerce of India belongs to English owners. If you trace the sale of a bale of Indian cotton exposed for sale in the Liverpool market, you will probably find that in all its successive stages, after being grown and picked by the native cultivator, it has been made ready and brought to the market by English capital and labour. An English agent has selected it in the producing district ; it has been carried down to the sea-coast by a railway company working with English capital ; an English mercantile firm in Bombay has pressed it, and sold the bill of exchange against it through an English broker to an English bank ; and it has been transported from Bombay to Liverpool on board an English steamer. So, again, with regard to the piece goods trade from this country, it is entirely financed and managed by Englishmen till the bales pass into the hands of the native dealers in the bazaar of Bombay. You will readily calculate how many different profits this vast trade which may be valued at a hundred millions sterling, yields to all these classes of English manufacturers, merchants, bankers, middlemen, shippers, engineers, and other mechanical experts. And when you add to such mercantile gains the private remittances sent home by English tradesmen and professional men settled in India, and by the civil and military servants of the Crown, you can realize how immense, in the aggregate, must be the contributions which our great dependency annually makes to the wealth of England. There is not a town, it may be said without exaggeration that there is not even a hamlet, in this country in which the fructifying influence of the capital thus acquired is not felt, although it may not be always recognised ; and I do not know any industry in the United Kingdom, small or great, which would not suffer loss, if the connection with India were broken off."

These are some of the benefits resulting to England from her connection with India. How the connection is appreciated by the native princes and people of India, even by those who, like Nepál, do not acknowledge the sovereignty of the Empress, has been made abundantly clear by the spontaneous offers of assistance which the mere threat of Russian invasion has evoked. Nothing is more manifest than that connection will be endangered if Russia be allowed to take Herát. We must not disguise from ourselves the fact that a loyalty which is fixed as long as we are victorious is not always proof against a long course of adversity. In his eloquent account of the fall of James II., Macaulay has described how the Prince who glibly uttered his '*est-ce possible*' as he learned the defection of one great noble after another, took an opportunity shortly afterwards of decamping himself. There remains, then, the great question—the question the most important of all—how to preserve Herát for Afghánistán. Before this all other questions sink into insignificance. In the presence of an enemy so unscrupulous it is a question beset with difficulties. The very act of repairing the crumbling walls of the town might, on the principle adopted by the wolf towards the lamb, be denounced by Russia as an act of hostility. Yet, at all hazards and with all speed it should be attempted; meanwhile, we must concentrate all our available troops in the Pishin valley, ready for a prompt advance.